Decoding 666
The Number of the Beast

The Magi Report Vol.1

ERIKA GREY

Copyright © 2016 ERIKA GREY

Library of Congress Control Number: 2016942225

All rights reserved.

ISBN:1940844088
ISBN-13:978-1940844084

DEDICATION

I dedicate this book to you dad who without you this report would not have been written.

CONTENTS

	Introduction	8
1	What is the Mark of the Beast	9
2	Bible Prophecy Predicts End Time Technological Breakthroughs	11
3	Antichrist Honors Technology god For Good Reason	13
4	The Mark of the Beast More Than Just A Payment Device	15
5	Key Mark of the Beast Passage in Bible Prophecy	17
6	The Image of the Beast is Here	20
7	The False Prophet's Fire From Heaven-A Holograph?	24
8	The Mark and Image of the Beast Guarantee Hell	26

9 Solving the Revelation 13:18 Riddle   29

   I.   Here is wisdom..................................29
   II.   For it is the number of a man.....................32
   III. Why a number for a name..........................33
   IV.   His number is 666................................40
   V.   666 is the ultimate idolatry.....................41
   VI.   The Beast-idolatry-currency and gold.............43
   VII. Numerology of gold represents the heavenly or
         idolatry..46

10 The Mark of the Beast Meets Geopolitics   49

11 The Seed of Satan & Immortality-Garden of Eden's DNA 53
   Changing Trees

   I.   The DNA changing tree of the knowledge of
         good and evil vs. tree of life...................54
   II.   The DNA changing tree of the knowledge of
         good and evil....................................57
   III. The seed of Satan-the change of man's DNA..58
   IV.   The serpent in the garden-a Satan possessed
         snake..59
   V.   When seed of Satan changed man's DNA Angel
         of Death and Hades
         appeared...60
   VI.   The tree of life supercharges man's DNA to
         immortality......................................61
   VII. Gold and DNA-its relation revealed in the
         garden of Eden...................................63
   VIII. Is the mark of the Beast a DNA change?..........63

12 Technology That Fits the Mark of the Beast   65

    I.   You'll have a choice between a brain or a hand chip..67
    II. Radio frequency tattoo eerily fits mark of the beast's description............................68
    III. Solving the riddle –counting the number of his name...69
    IV. Jesus warns of life in the Antichrist's police state 70
    V.   The Antichrist will give you two choices for the mark..73

13 The Image of the Beast-The Siege of Jerusalem   75

    I.   Run from the mark of the Beast to the mountains...79
    II. Mass betrayals against those who refuse to take the mark of the Beast.........................81
    III. Torture and death for those who don't take the mark of the Beast.............................82
    IV. 1290 days of Daniel-30 days of bowl judgements 84
    V.   Possible reasons for the battle of Armageddon 86
    VI. The cataclysmic end of the world and return of Christ...87

14. The Technology god In the Book of Daniel   88

    I.   The technology god and it's prophets...........89
    II. The technology gods teachings, buzzwords and mark of the Beast..........................91
    III. Miracles duplicated by technology god..........93

15 The Technology Tower of Babel   95

    I. Two towers of Babel that reach to the Heavens
       CERN and FAST..............…..……....98
    II. The Antichrist will head technology Tower of
       Babel………………………………..100
    III. Funding For Babel's mark of the Beast in place
       ………………………………………..100

16 Parallel Dimensions   103

    I. Parallel Universe-The God of the Bible….…104
    II. Parallel Universe-demons and angels in the
       Revelation……………………………..106
    III. Parallel Universe-understood by a child….…108
    IV. The Parallel dimension connects with the
       physical world…………………………109
    V. Antichrist via technology will mimic the Holy
       Trinity………………………………….110

17 Quantum Computers-666 the Image and Mark of the   113
    Beast

    I. D-Wave and Demons-The Bible-Demons are in
       the idols……………………………….114
    II. Quantum Computers-its link to Satan and 666
       ………………………………………...116
    III. Nebuchadnezzar's Image of Cubits Vs.
       Quantum Computer's Qubits……………117
    IV. IV. The Revelation's Fractal Sequence -777 vs.
       666 and Quantum Computing……………117

18 Taking the Mark of the Beast-The Unforgivable Sin of   120
    Blasphemy Against the Holy Spirit

    I.   Abomination of Desolation-Blasphemy of the Holy Spirit..................................123
    II. The Mysterious Restrainer Removed Via Blasphemy of the Holy Spirit...........125
    III. 666 The Number of Blasphemy of the Holy Spirit......................................126

BIBLIOGRAPHY   128

ERIKA GREY

FOR ARTICLES, BOOKS, REPORTS AND VIDEOS FROM ERIKA GREY GO TO:

www.erikagrey.com

Introduction-A Time Like No Other

No other passages in Scripture has been more talked about in end time Bible prophecy than those dealing with the mark of the Beast. In decoding the mark, some of the Bible's deepest mysteries are revealed. In this report the passages dealing with the mark of the Beast are decoded as much as possible as one can unravel them in looking forward to a time that is yet future but not far off.

As the technologies have advanced they have helped to provide the full meaning of the prophetic Scriptures that relate to technological advances. There are a few areas that remain grey and these are highlighted in this commentary. This work provides a detailed analysis and status report of the mark of the Beast and its road to fulfillment. It is based on a good deal of research from government entity's to leading university's and renown publications.

What stands out is how close we are to the start of the Tribulation. If you are a Christian, there is little time left to serve the Savior. If you do not know Jesus Christ as your personal savior, now is the time to know Him to escape the horrors of what lies ahead.

In case you are not familiar with end time Bible prophecy, the prophetic writings in Scripture takes you into the throne room of the Almighty God and you see a glimpse of Him like you do not see anywhere else in the Bible. Bible prophecy crosses the time and dimension barriers. What becomes evident is the Spiritual world and its warfare. The battle of the ages, which ends at Armageddon. You see the many parallels of Jesus and the Antichrist and these culminate during the reign of the Antichrist and with the implementation of the mark of the Beast

The time will be like none other, as along with the unleashing of God's judgements, the world is under the rule of the very son Satan himself. The only man in the Bible with a number for a his name and for reasons revealed in this report.

If you are living during the early Tribulation and have come across this report, may it give you all the information that you are seeking.

1
What is the Mark of the Beast?

During the Tribulation, which is the seven year period of judgements predicted in Bible prophecy that ends with the battle of Armageddon and the second coming of Jesus Christ, Satan attempts to establish his kingdom here on the earth through a dictator known in evangelical circles as the Antichrist. He is used by God to judge the world for its sin. During his reign the Antichrist will implement a system by which no man can buy or sell unless he wears a mark placed on his forehead or wrist. This etching in one's flesh represents the Beast that is the Antichrist, or 666. It will provide him ultimate control in his police state.

Bible scholars theorized before the recent technological strides of the last decade that the mark would be part of a high-tech system that eliminated cash for the buying of goods. The Antichrist institutes this system midway through the Tribulation. He launches it as both a technological breakthrough and a prerequisite for life in his totalitarian regime. Revelation refers to the mark in a spiritual context. Whosoever receives it spends eternity in hell.

The mark of the Beast prediction this last century was out of touch with the times. Writers noted the tattooing and numbering of prisoners at Auschwitz concentration camps during World War II to illustrate a use that fit the era. This all changed in 1985 with the advent of the information and telecommunications revolution. From about 1990 onward we have seen a major spike upward in end time signs.

Never before in history have we seen Bible prophecy literally unfold before our eyes. The technologies which could fulfil the mark of the Beast prophecy are now in existence.

2

Bible Prophecy Predicts End Time-Technological Breakthroughs

In the book of Daniel, the prophet is told of the technological breakthroughs at the time of the end. In Daniel 12:4 it states, "But you, Daniel, shut up the words, and seal the book until the time of the end; many shall run to and fro, and knowledge shall increase."

Many running to and fro describes modern transportation, airplanes, cars and trains. The word for knowledge used in this verse for increase in the Hebrew means, "increase exceedingly, enlarge, become numerous, become many, multiply, to make great', plenty. It also means to grow up. This describes the machine and finally this technological age, which are the end times and provide the framework for the fulfillment of various prophecies.

Adding impetus to the rapid expansion in knowledge are the funding by nations to pursue the economic growth that new technologies can spur. From computers to television, consumers want the latest features. This fact has increased growth and spending in commercial research and development programs by, the US, China, the EU and Japan. This means that nations are in a race to promote new technological breakthroughs, and they work hard at making and selling the latest products.

The European Union jumped on this bandwagon in as early as 1974. Today, scientific research is the third largest area of EU spending, after agriculture and structural development. The Federal Trust for Education and Research, a think-tank organization that aids in formulating EU policy, stated several decades ago in a report that:

Europe cannot afford to exclude itself from the profound technological transformation which is currently sweeping the world and which is expected to be the locomotive of economic development over the next two or three decades. Historians have noted that, periodically, the world brings forth a new technology, or group of related technologies, of such a revolutionary nature that it transforms the whole basis of economic activity...There is little disagreement that information technology is the mainstream technology of the current era.

In this quest, the mark of the Beast will be researched and launched.

3

The Antichrist Honors the Technology god For Good Reason

Daniel 11:37-39 states of the Antichrist:

37 He shall regard neither the God of his fathers nor the desire of women, nor regard any god; for he shall exalt himself above them all. 38 But in their place he shall honor a god of fortresses; and a god which his fathers did not know he shall honor with gold and silver, with precious stones and pleasant things. 39 Thus he shall act against the strongest fortresses with a foreign god, which he shall acknowledge, and advance its glory; and he shall cause them to rule over many, and divide the land for gain.

The Antichrist will establish himself as a god, but based on this verse he will honor a god of forces or fortresses, which his fathers did not know. This is technology because these advances did not exist in the day of his fathers. Forces from the Hebrew means a rock, strong place, place of safety, stronghold, which is what technology will provide to the Antichrist's police state. From drones, cameras, GPS tracking, invisible cloaks in which military personal cannot be seen, or technology that can find living people behind walls to missile detection and destruction, Technology provides a super fortress as well as a super weapon, which is why the verse tells us he acts against the strongest fortresses with this god.

The King James Bible specifies *"in his estate"* meaning in his office or during his tenure of his presidency. *"He will cause them to rule"* in the Hebrew it means cause to rule to exercise dominion, which is exactly how he will use technology and his mark for his police state.

The Antichrist's use of technology goes beyond using it to control the masses, he brings it to its height of evil and for a use that could only be conceived in the pits of hell and from Satan himself. The Antichrist and the latest technologies go hand in hand as he will use technology to glorify himself and to mimic God. This is why he honors it with gold and silver, precious stones and pleasant things. This being interpreted, he will use money, taxpayer money's via governmental monies to fund the technologies that help him achieve his diabolical aims.

4

The Mark of the Beast- More Than Just A Payment Device

Evangelical Christians knew that the mark of the Beast would be a high tech method of buying and selling and it became big news when there came talk of a cash less society and credit and debit cards became the norm.

In around the year 2000, emerged from the tech world identification implants, called sub-dermal implants,(Verichip, RFID chip) which marketed to pet owners to identify their lost pets and is also used for medical purposes and to track criminals. It was literally right out of the book of Revelation and the Evangelical Christian community spread the news like a wild fire.

The mark of the Beast causes one to spend their eternity in hell. God is not going to send anyone to hell over a payment system, even one that requires a subdermal chip.

In Revelation we are told in several passages that anyone who takes the mark of the Beast will go to hell. This mark is more than a payment system to cause one to lose their chance at heaven and damn them to hell.

The Antichrist's kingdom is a counterfeit to the kingdom of God. We see many parallels in Scripture of the Antichrist to Jesus. God marks those who are His and the Antichrist also will mark those who belong to him.

The device the Scripture forecasts is more than just a payment device. How do we get God's mark? By trusting in Jesus as our Savior, by making Him first in our life by worshiping Him as savior. The Holy Spirit connects us with God. The mark of the Beast will be the technological counterpart.

There are six verses about the mark and in them we read that those who take the mark also worship the image of the Beast. This worship and the taking of the mark go together.

You cannot buy or sell if you do not have the mark and so we know that the mark of the Beast will also act as a payment device, but a payment device should not cause one to go to hell should it? This is because it is more than just a payment device. There is good reason why the mark of the Beast causes eternal damnation and this also helps in decoding the mark of the Beast and finding the technology that fits it.

5
Key Mark of the Beast Passage in Bible Prophecy

The key mark of the Beast passage is Revelation Chapter 13. All other Bible verses in both the Old and New Testament provide additional information that builds upon this passage.

In this chapter we learn that a Beast rises from the sea and this is the empire that the Antichrist leads. Its seven heads, ten horns, resemblance to a leopard, feet of a bear, and mouth of a lion compare to the Beast described in the book of Daniel. The ten horns are ten kings, which the book of Daniel also identified and this gives us a view to the empire's institutional structure. The book of Daniel gives us a time frame of 42 months and we see the same time span here in Revelation Chapter 13. This is the second half of the Tribulation known as the Great Tribulation.

The Antichrist will receive a head wound and come back to life and it is at this time that Satan enters his body and he goes into the Holy of Holies in the Jewish temple- that is going to be rebuilt- and declares that he is god. He places an abominable thing in the Holy of Holies, which will most likely be his cloned image, which will be discussed in detail in this report. It is at this time the Antichrist institutes his mark on all people, via technology and he initiates the ultimate police state. I have established in my book, *The Seat of the Antichrist: Bible Prophecy and the European Union* that the EU is the Beast of Revelation that will launch the Antichrist.

Revelation Chapter 13 reads:

13 Then I stood on the sand of the sea. And I saw a beast rising up out of the sea, having seven heads and ten horns, and on his horns ten crowns, and on his heads a blasphemous name. ² Now the beast which I saw was like a leopard, his feet were like the feet of a bear, and his mouth like the mouth of a lion. The dragon gave him his power, his throne, and great authority. ³ And I saw one of his heads as if it had been mortally wounded, and his deadly wound was healed. And all the world marveled and followed the beast. ⁴ So they worshiped the dragon who gave authority to the beast; and they worshiped the beast, saying, "Who is like the beast? Who is able to make war with him?"

⁵ And he was given a mouth speaking great things and blasphemies, and he was given authority to continue for forty-two months. ⁶ Then he opened his mouth in blasphemy against God, to blaspheme His name, His tabernacle, and those who dwell in heaven. ⁷ It was granted to him to make war with the saints and to overcome them. And authority was given him over every tribe, tongue, and nation. ⁸ All who dwell on the earth will worship him, whose names have not been written in the Book of Life of the Lamb slain from the foundation of the world.

¹¹ Then I saw another beast coming up out of the earth, and he had two horns like a lamb and spoke like a dragon. ¹² And he exercises all the authority of the first beast in his presence, and causes the earth and those who dwell in it to worship the first beast, whose deadly wound was healed. ¹³ He performs great signs, so that he even makes fire come down from heaven on the earth in the sight of men. ¹⁴ And he deceives those who dwell on the earth by those signs which he was granted to do in the sight of the beast, telling those who dwell on the earth to make an image to the beast who was wounded by the sword and lived. ¹⁵ He was granted power to give breath to the image of the beast, that the image of the beast should both speak and cause as many as would not worship the image of the beast to be killed. ¹⁶ He causes all, both small and great, rich and poor, free and slave, to receive a mark on their right hand or on their foreheads, ¹⁷ and that no one may buy or sell except one who has the mark or the name of the beast, or the number of his name.

¹⁸ Here is wisdom. Let him who has understanding calculate the number of the beast, for it is the number of a man: His number is 666.

The passage begins with describing the government of the beast and transitions to the person also called the beast. Satan's dominion over both the Antichrist and his empire is established and also presents the leading entity in the unholy trinity. From there we learn of his fatal wound, which Zechariah 11:17 tells us will leave his right eye blinded and his arm paralyzed.

The Bible informs us of the Antichrist's resurrection, his establishing that he is a deity, and his war with the Saints. In this chapter we see the appearance of the third member of the unholy trinity, his miracles and his commissioning the making of the image of the Beast, His power to give the breath of life to the image and then the decree that all who do not worship the image of the beast will be put to death and simultaneously with this worship he causes all to take the name of the beast or number of the beast's name. The passage then concludes with the Bible's most mysterious and frightening riddle to count the number of the name of the beast and the number of the man is 666.

6

The Image of The Beast is Here

In the book of Revelation the image of the Beast always precedes the mark of the Beast. Revelation 13:18 is the only place the mark is mentioned without a reference to the image and this is because it provides the riddle that elaborates on the identity of the Beast. In all other Bible verses concerning the mark of the Beast we see the triad of the worship of the beast, his image and taking the mark. In one verse the mark is referred to as the number of his name.

The image of the beast precedes the Mark of the Beast and is equal with the mark. Evangelical Christian end time watchers and theologians pay the image of the beast little attention, yet it is tied to and part of the triad of the mark of the Beast.

What is frightening is that not only does the technology exist for the mark of the Beast but also for the image of the beast as well. Never before in history has a technology launched that fits the image of the Beast to its very description than today.

The 2045.com project brings together leading scientists from all over the world to achieve the creation of an artificial human body and transfer human consciousness to it. They believe that by 2045 they will achieve such a body that will surpass our bodies in terms of functionality and this body will be capable of withstanding extreme conditions and can initially be operated remotely.

The 2045 project is man's attempt at duplicating the glorified bodies that are promised in the Bible. On their website is an immortality button and when you push it you read:

Imperfect biological bodies
...depend on temperature, pressure, oxygen and other environmental conditions;
...depend on food and water:
...get sick easily;
...limit the development of our planet;
...all eventually die.

The 2045 Initiative Solution
Self-directed evolution through partial and complete replacement of your biological body with an artificial avatar.
60% of the technology is already available
40% will be developed over the next 3 decades
Avatar R&D Network run by top experts

Personal avatar development capability is available today. From there you can select a remote control avatar (Avatar A) that the website states is 85% complete and will be available in the next 3 years. This avatar would be good for disabled persons, business tele-travel and first responders.

Avatar B is a full body prosthesis and will have a man's head transplanted onto it. They project it will be completed in 5 to 7 years, Avatar C with a super human body featuring greater than human capabilities, an artificial brain and the transferal of human consciousness. This one is 20 to 25 years until completion but can be accelerated if there is increased investment of dollars into the research. On this website you can commission the building of your own personal avatar for 3 million dollars.

Man's attempt to achieve immortality is a waste of time and resources because the way to achieve immortality is promised in the Bible.

Satan caused the fall of man along with disease and death and now through technology Satan offers his counterfeit to what God has offered for free in the Bible. God's cost for eternal life is too high a price for many because it requires faith in the finished work of Jesus Christ and belief in Him as the Son of God.

Scientists also believe through DNA engineering and Brain Chips they can perfect man's body and help it to achieve superhuman traits.

Technology has become a tower of Babel and it currently exists alongside its geopolitical counterpart of world federalism, which unites the world via world institutions and regional trade blocks.

Scientists are attempting to achieve a status of being on par with God and perfecting his creation, such as making bunny rabbits glow in the dark, creating human skin that is tough as Kevlar made from goats that produce silk in their milk from their DNA being merged with spider DNA.

Man is hoping to eradicate disease and with brain technology upload his memory, improve eyesight, give a human body night vision and special hearing capabilities.

In this current tech environment now exists a perfect parallel with the image of the Beast of Revelation 13. We can now easily speculate on the finer details.

What is astounding is that not only does the technology exist for the image of the beast but we can also know what will not be achieved and what will be accomplished through a miracle of God. This is how close we are to the Rapture and how far along we are in the end times.

Based on Revelation 13, the 2045 project will achieve creating a duplicate robotic body of the Antichrist. This matches the image of the Beast. The first avatar is going to be a robotic body that is controlled remotely, they believe by 2030 to 2035 they will be able to transfer a human personality or human consciousness into the avatar.

This will not be achieved as they think, the False Prophet comes in and he might not be a religious leader as we have anticipated, he might be a scientist and he will according to Scripture give breath to the image of the beast, but this is a power given to him by God, for the Bible tells us in Revelation 13:15, *"He was granted to give breath to the image of the beast, that the image of the beast should both speak and cause as many as would not worship it to be killed."*

Based on this verse the image of the beast is an avatar that looks identical to the Antichrist, and the False Prophet is granted by God to give it breath. In Genesis 2:7 we see God giving Adam the breath of life, but notice here the False Prophet can only give it breath but not the breath of life. The Antichrist's look alike avatar or robot will receive consciousness but only by way and permission of God granting that power, and this can come in the form of a technological achievement, but it is not alive in the way humans are alive, but more like an animal is alive. The consciousness allows the image, i.e. avatar to speak and deceives many that man has now achieved immortality in this robot, but it is the Antichrist who shows off his immortality via his image. It should also be noted that the Beast and the False Prophet are thrown into the lake of fire, but not the image of the Beast because it is not given a soul, it is given breath, which is what animals, birds and reptiles are given, but not a soul.

It is my assessment based on the personality of the Antichrist that the avatar will be made for him alone and these avatars will not be made for others as he claims to be God and now reveals his immortality through the avatar.

The avatar will stand in the Holy of Holies and will be worshipped. It is also a possibility that the Christians who do not worship the image or take the mark of the Beast will be beheaded within the Third Temple on the alter intended for animal sacrifices.

The image of the Beast's avatar or robot, will also have some super capabilities discussed in detail in a later chapter in this report.

7

The False Prophet's Fire From Heaven A Holograph?

Revelation 13:13-15 states:

"He performs great signs, so that he even makes fire come down from heaven on the earth in the sight of men. [14] *And he deceives those who dwell on the earth by those signs which he was granted to do in the sight of the beast, telling those who dwell on the earth to make an image to the beast who was wounded by the sword and lived.* [15] *He was granted power to give breath to the image of the beast, that the image of the beast should both speak and cause as many as would not worship the image of the beast to be killed."*

In addition to breathing life into the image of the Beast, we see other miracles that the False Prophet accomplishes and one of these includes making fire come down from heaven in the sight of men. While this might very well be a miracle it also sounds like advanced holographic technology, which allows people to see and feel objects from other parts of the world. It also gives individuals the ability to appear on stage and speak to people who are miles away in another room. Holographic technology can allow the appearance of fire from heaven. There are also other 3 D virtual reality technologies in the works, that can also cause these type of spectacles. Another area is haptic communication or HMI's human to machine interaction that would allow one to go to an online web store and have the ability to touch a product before buying it. This technology would also be used for video conferencing where family members can interact "haptically" while away from each other, according to Professor Eckehard Steinback in the interview, "Touch and Feel Over Distance: The Next Trend in ICT.?" They are in the process of how to commercialize selected results and get an idea of market potential and produce prototypes for potential customers. Combined with holographic technology one would be able to feel the heat from the holographic flame the Antichrist produces.

Considering where technology is heading, that it is a Tower of Babel where man believes he can be like God, even to the point of thinking he can perfect on God's creation, and knowing that the Antichrist honors the god of technology, the False Prophet may not be a religious leader as Evangelicals have assumed but might be a scientist advocating the latest Tower of Babel technologies that support the claimed deity of the Antichrist.

It might be that the miracles the Bible speaks of in Revelation 13 are not miracles like Jesus performed, but technological feats and accomplishments which appear as miracles. The word for miracles used in Revelation 13 means a sign, mark, token and "that by which a person or a thing is distinguished from others and is known," or "a sign, prodigy, portent, i.e. an usual occurrence transcending the common course of nature." This could fit technological achievements and the direction it is moving towards and fulfil the miracles performed by the False Prophet in Revelation 13.

8

The Mark and Image of the Beast Guarantee Hell

Once the image of the Beast is commissioned, made and set up we see the mark of the Beast instituted.

The phrase, "that the image of the beast should both speak and cause as many as would not worship the image of the Beast to be killed," indicates that it is the image of the Beast that causes death. Somehow the Antichrist's avatar or robot will have greater capabilities than just being a human like clone of the Antichrist, but might serve another purpose and be connected to the cloud and act to connect to a data center.

All of the world cannot go to the place the image of the Beast stands to worship it, the worship of the image is the action of taking the mark of the Beast, which is connected to the image.

Before we go further it must be stated again that the mark of the Beast is always in conjunction with worship of the image of the Beast. We see in Revelation 13 that the image of the Beast is joined with the mark of the Beast and these together are taken and guarantee hell for the recipient.

"*^{15} He was granted power to give breath to the image of the beast, that the image of the beast should both speak and cause as many as would not worship the image of the beast to be killed. ^{16} He causes all, both small and great, rich and poor, free and slave, to receive a mark on their right hand or on their foreheads, ^{17} and that no one may buy or sell except one who has the mark or the name of the beast, or the number of his name."*

Revelation 14:9-11 reads:

^{9} "Then a third angel followed them, saying with a loud voice, "If anyone worships the beast and his image, and receives his mark on his forehead or on his hand, ^{10} he himself shall also drink of the wine of the wrath of God, which is poured out full strength into the cup of His indignation. He shall be tormented with fire and brimstone in the presence of the holy angels and in the presence of the Lamb. ^{11} And the smoke of their torment ascends forever and ever; and they have no rest day or night, who worship the beast and his image, and whoever receives the mark of his name."

In Revelation 14:11 once again, we see the triad of the mark of the Beast tied with worshiping the Beast, his image and receiving the mark. Revelation 14:11 affirms:

^{11} "And the smoke of their torment ascends forever and ever; and they have no rest day or night, who worship the beast and his image, and whoever receives the mark of his name."

We see from these verses that the Beast, his image and the mark are all in sync. We will keep this in mind as we go further to decode the riddle of Revelation 13:18.

Worshiping the Beast means worshiping the Antichrist, his kingdom or government, his image and receiving the mark. They are each tied in one to another. The image of the Beast is the result of a technological achievement and by it the Antichrist reveals his immortality.

There is the possibility that the image is not tied directly with the mark of the Beast acting as a mainframe computer connected to the cloud and the mark, which is a chip. It could be that the completion of the avatar is the proof man needs that the Antichrist achieved immortality is through technology and in this belief they take the mark of the Beast. The Antichrist after the completion of his image, makes everyone take the mark or the number of his name.

In this report I present both possibilities, but lean toward the image of the Beast directly tied to the mark of the Beast. It is the worship of all three that causes one to spend eternity in hell, and why it guarantees hell is revealed in this report.

9
Solving the Revelation 13:18 Riddle

I. Here is Wisdom

No other passage has mystified than Revelation 13:18: *"Here is wisdom Let him who has understanding count the number of the beast, for it is the number of a man and his number is 666."*

There are two riddles in the Bible and both are in the book of Revelation and deal with the Antichrist. Revelation 17:9-11 provides a riddle which identifies the government of the Antichrist and Revelation 13:18 provides a mystery that identifies the Antichrist himself via his mark. Both puzzles reveal deep Scriptural truths in solving them.

Aside from the two challenges that occur in the book of Revelation there is a riddle given is Judges 14:2-18, but it was posed by Samson and not by Christ Himself. While all of the Revelation and the book of Daniel provide visions and explanation's to the dreams, Revelation 13:18 deviates to posing to the reader a difficult and complex riddle, more challenging than the one posed in Revelation 17:9, which has been solved. For reference see my article, "The Identity of the 7th and 8th Head of Revelation Explained."

We are given our first hint in the verse before verse 18. *⁷ And that no man might buy or sell, save he that had the mark, or the name of the beast, or the number of his name.* We learn that the number and the name of the beast are one in the same.

Many believe that the riddle will easily be solved by counting the name of the Antichrist and that his number in the Hebrew or English language will add up to 666, thus identifying him. The riddle is much more difficult and has more deeper meaning than just calculating the number of a man based on his name, although you will count to solve it. To decode the riddle we are going to look at it phrase by phrase. It begins with, *"Here is wisdom."*

It should be noted that the riddle in Revelation 17 also begins with a similar phrase of *"here is the mind that has wisdom."* Each time wisdom is mentioned in the Bible it refers to either great intellectual capacity or the ability to understand deep spiritual truths.

Great Intellectual Capability

The prophet Daniel served in three of the four world empires because of his keen intellect but he also possessed the ability to understand deep spiritual truths. The Antichrist we are told will possess a keen intellect and his intelligence is referred to as wisdom. By it he will lead his government.

The Bible makes mention of kings consulting their wise men, which was another word for advisors and consultants. The Magi or Wise Men were analysts who studied astrology, science and the prophetic word and through their understanding of each were able to from two Bible verses come to the exact location of the birth place of Jesus Christ. Like the prophet Daniel they also received visions so their intellect also crossed into possessing spiritual wisdom.

Godly Wisdom

Proverbs 9:10 states, *"The fear of the Lord is the beginning of wisdom and the knowledge of the holy is understanding."* Godly wisdom is understanding Biblical teachings of God and of His son Jesus Christ. Knowledge of the holy is understanding the deeper principles and mysteries in the word of God that center around His holiness. Holiness is not piety but rather separation from the ways of the world, to serve an esoteric God whose ways and whose world is incomprehensible to the finite mind. We accept it none-the-less.

Revelation's **Here is wisdom** is a loaded phrase because what it is telling you is that this riddle pertains to Godly wisdom, which means a deeper Biblical teaching that is not normally found, that one would have to think about.

While the word wisdom is used in many instances in the Bible we never see the phrase, "*Here is wisdom*". Here in the Greek means *to this place,* and takes skill to understand. We see wisdom and understanding in Proverbs relating to spiritual wisdom, we also see it pertaining to intellect as with the prophet Daniel, whose skill caused him to serve chief roles within the governments of three of the four world empires that existed.

Our next phrase is **"Let him who has understanding"** meaning that to decode Revelation 13:18 it will not only take wisdom in uncovering Biblical mysteries but also specialized skill. We see "understanding" used in Scripture denoting specialized skill. We find wisdom and understanding used 53 times in the Bible and each time one is a component of the other meaning that they are two separate parts but belong together. Someone can have understanding without wisdom and wisdom without understanding. Knowledge is different than wisdom and understanding in the Bible. Wisdom is comparable to aptitude.

We see this phrase the most referring to the prophet Daniel, which book parallels with the book of Revelation. Only instead of Revelation 13:18 telling us about the prophet Daniel's wisdom, it now poses the riddle to those who are out there who have studied the prophetic books to help them decode the riddle. We actually see wisdom and understanding in relation to the prophet Daniel used three times in Chapter 1. There is a another key verse in the Bible that uses the phrase wisdom and understanding that I will present after we first look into the verse further.

In the book of Daniel in reference to the persecution of the Tribulation saints, we see their having this wisdom and understanding and this too is discussed in more detail later in this report.

II. Solving the Revelation 13:18 Riddle : the Beast- For It is The Number of A Man

We are told in this next phrase that decoding the riddle will take a calculation of the number of the Beast so our next question is what is the Beast because in the beginning of Revelation 13 we see the description of an empire and then a man. So we go to the next phrase.

For it is the number of a man

This phrase is where many looking to decode the riddle err. Once they read it is the number of a man they only look at the man and thus the hypothesis of counting the number of his name. What they fail to see if that the man is one with his empire such as Adolph Hitler and the Third Reich. In history they do not exist without the other and it is the same for future events. After the description of the empire in the early part of Revelation 13, we see the emergence of a man in verse 5. It states, *"and he was given a mouth speaking great things."* We see this theme in the dream image in Daniel regarding Babylon.

As Daniel begins to interpret Nebuchadnezzar's dream, which depicts the prophetic image of the four world empires that will impact the nation of Israel. Daniel tells us that the first is Babylon and Daniel informs Nebuchadnezzar that he is this first kingdom. *"But after you shall arise another kingdom inferior to yours."* (Daniel 2:39).

We see later when Daniel interprets Nebuchadnezzar's dream in Daniel 4:22, he states to Nebuchadnezzar, *"It is you O king who have grown and become strong; for your greatness has grown and reaches to the heavens and your dominion to the end of the earth."*

It was Babylon that became great under Nebuchadnezzar. We see a similar scenario for the Antichrist. The book of Daniel predicts concerning his empire, Daniel 8:9-10 reads, *"And out of one of them came a little horn which grew exceedingly great toward the south, toward the east, and toward the Glorious Land. And it grew up to the host of heaven…"*

We see this again the image of the final world empire synonymous with an empire or morphing into a man in Daniel Chapter 7:7-8:

"After this I saw in the night visions, and behold, a fourth beast, dreadful and terrible. Exceedingly strong .It had huge iron teeth; it was devouring, breaking in pieces and trampling the residue with its feet. It was different from all the beasts that were before it and it had ten horns.

I was considering the horns and there was another horn a little horn before whom three of the first horns were plucked up by the roots. And there in this horn were eyes like the eyes of a man and a mouth speaking pompous words."

So we have established that the Antichrist and his empire are one in the same. The Beast is both the man and his empire. The EU is the final world empire, and the future EU under the leadership of the Antichrist. The EU in its final form under the headship of Antichrist is the Beast of Revelation. So when one looks to decode the number of the Beast, it is a number that is related to his empire as well, i.e. to the EU.

III. Solving the Revelation 13:18 Riddle : Antichrist- Why A Number for A Name

We get a major clue in the verse before which states: *And that no man might buy or sell, save he that had the mark, or the name of the beast, or the number of his name,*

What we learn about the number of the man is that it is also his name.

Nowhere in Scripture is anyone named with a number. It appears as if this verse does not belong because of this fact. This is the only place where a man is named a number and we have to ask why?

The answer is deep in the Scriptures. Bible scholars know that you must be able to compare Scripture with Scripture to form a doctrine. Anyone can take Bible verses and passages and give them a meaning, but if a teaching cannot be backed up with Scripture then it is not Bible doctrine.

When we look at why a number is given for the Antichrist's name we discover a deeper, hidden biblical truth and what this means for those living during the Tribulation under the Antichrist's reign.

The meaning of number in the Bible is dimensional and has a spiritual meaning that gives us a glimpse into the spiritual world.
The prophetic writings not only disclose future events but take us into the throne room of God; depicted in Revelation, Ezekiel and Isaiah, which are all prophetic books. In delving into prophecy you learn more than any place else of the spiritual world and of the ways of God Himself. You will see this as I further reveal the spiritual significance of why the Antichrist has a number for a name.

We get our first hint in Exodus 30:11-16:

[11] Then the LORD spoke to Moses, saying:
[12] "When you take the census of the children of Israel for their number, then every man shall give a ransom for himself to the LORD, when you number them, that there may be no plague among them when you number them.
[13] This is what everyone among those who are numbered shall give: half a shekel according to the shekel of the sanctuary (a shekel is twenty gerahs). The half-shekel shall be an offering to the LORD.
[14] Everyone included among those who are numbered, from twenty years old and above, shall give an offering to the LORD.
[15] The rich shall not give more and the poor shall not give less than half a shekel, when you give an offering to the LORD, to make atonement for yourselves.
[16] And you shall take the atonement money of the children of Israel, and shall appoint it for the service of the tabernacle of meeting, that it may be a memorial for the children of Israel before the LORD, to make atonement for yourselves."

Notice that if a man was to be numbered or counted, he had to pay a ransom and to make atonement, which looked to Jesus who became the ransom for many and the atonement for men's souls. We see here that if a man is numbered he is essentially damned. Even those who do the numbering can bring on a plague if a ransom is not given. Thus being numbered is associated with spiritual death.

In 2 Samuel 24 we read the account where Satan tempted David to number Israel. The story is also told in 1 Chronicles 21. This is the first mention of Satan by name in the Old Testament. In the first mention of Satan by name he has tempted David to number Israel and this numbering occurred without the ransom and God judged David's sin harshly.

2 Samuel 24:1-2 tells us:

24 "Again the anger of the LORD was aroused against Israel, and He moved David against them to say, "Go, number Israel and Judah."
² So the king said to Joab the commander of the army who was with him, "Now go throughout all the tribes of Israel, from Dan to Beersheba, and count the people, that I may know the number of the people."

David knew that he sinned in 2 Samuel 24:10 it states:

¹⁰ "And David's heart condemned him after he had numbered the people. So David said to the LORD, "I have sinned greatly in what I have done; but now, I pray, O LORD, take away the iniquity of Your servant, for I have done very foolishly."

God gave David the choice on which judgement to choose, either seven years of famine, three months of running from his enemies or three days of plagues and David chose three days of plagues and 70 thousand men died. (2 Samuel 24:11).

David got the plague to end by erecting an alter on the threshing floor and offering burnt offerings and peace offerings. (2 Samuel 24:18-24).

We see this negative connotation with being numbered in Isaiah 53:12 concerning Jesus, it reads, *"Therefore will I divide Him a portion with the great, and He shall divide the spoil with the strong because He poured out His soul unto death, And He was numbered with the transgressors."*

Jesus was numbered with the transgressors for death, the death that sin causes and the resulting separation from God. 2 Corinthians 5:21 confirms, *"For He made Him who knew no sin to be sin for us, that we might become the righteousness of God in Him.* Jesus for that time on the cross was numbered along with the transgressors as He took their sin upon Him.

In the Hebrew the word for numbered is manah and it means:

To count, number, assign, tell, appoint, prepare.
To be counted, be numbered,
To be reckoned, be assigned,
To appoint, ordain,
Appointed, participate.

From the definition we see that being numbered takes on another meaning of being appointed and assigned.

We are beginning to get the picture that those who are numbered have no redemption for their souls and are appointed to hell's fires. Jesus himself becomes numbered with the transgressors as he became the atonement for sin.

We also see this negative connotation for numbered in Daniel 5:26 concerning the end of the Babylonian kingdom when Belshazzar the son of Nebuchadnezzar was having a feast and using the temple cups and utensils for his party when a large hand came and wrote some writing on the wall. Daniel was called to interpret the writing and he stated: *"This is the interpretation of each word. MENE: God has numbered your kingdom, and finished it.*

The word men-aw in the Aramaic means to count, appoint:— number, ordain, set. Again we see the term numbered meaning appointed to death. We also see this teaching in those who take the Mark of the Beast will be damned to hell via taking the Antichrist's number vs. the name of Christ, they number themselves for death.

The mark of the Beast is mentioned twice in the Revelation and referenced to in six verses.

A key verse that mentions eternal damnation for taking the mark or the number of the Antichrist's name is Revelation 14:9-11 and it reads:

Then a third angel followed them, saying with a loud voice, "If anyone worships the beast and his image, and receives his mark on his forehead or on his hand, he himself shall also drink of the wine of the wrath of God, which is poured out full strength into the cup of His indignation. He shall be tormented with fire and brimstone in the presence of the holy angels and in the presence of the Lamb. ¹¹ And the smoke of their torment ascends forever and ever; and they have no rest day or night, who worship the beast and his image, and whoever receives the mark of his name..

We see this in God's promise to Abraham a double meaning for numbered in Genesis when God promised him that that his descendants will be as the dust of the earth which cannot be numbered.

Jeremiah 33: 22, *As the host of heaven cannot be numbered , neither the sand of the sea measured: so will I multiply the seed of David my servant, and the Levites that minister unto me.*

Hosea 1:10 states, *"Yet the number of the children of Israel shall be as the sand of the sea, which cannot be measured nor numbered and it shall come to pass that in the place where it is said unto the, ye are not my people, there it shall be said unto them, ye are the sons of the living God."*

While the promise describes the amount of Abraham's descendants that are innumerable, many believed that this was why when David numbered the Israelites he defied God because of this passage. There was also the idea floated that because David was looking to the number of his army and not to God, but in the book of Numbers the numbers are recorded. Numbering needed to follow a protocol signifying redemption for the numbered. Why? Because those who are numbered are damned. When you are numbered you are appointed to death. When you are given a name you are redeemed and your name is written in the book of life.

What we glean from Revelation 13:18 is that if you are not given a name, and your name is not written in the book of life but if you are numbered meaning you are appointed for death, i.e. eternal death and damnation.

Revelation 22:4 states, *"And they shall see his face and his name shall be in their foreheads."*

In these two verses we see that the redeemed are given a name, in contrast to the damned that are numbered. We also see the connection between those whose names are written in the book of life. These persons are not numbered. Consider the following verses:

Philippians 4:3 And I intreat thee also, true yoke fellow help those women which labored with me in the gospel, with Clement also, and with other my fellow labourers, whose names are written in the book of life.

Revelation 3:5 He that overcometh, the same shall be clothed in white raiment and I will not blot out his name out of the book of life, but I will confess his name before my Father, and before his angels.

Revelation 13:18 And all that dwell upon the earth shall worship him, whose names are not written in the book of life of the Lamb slain from the foundation of the world.

Revelation 17:18 The beast that thou sawest was and is not; and shall ascend out of the bottomless pit, and go into perdition: and they that dwell on the earth shall wonder, whose names were not written in the book of life from the foundation of the world, when they behold the beast that was, and is not, and yet is.

Revelation 20:15 And whosoever was not found written in the book of life was cast into the lake of fire.

Revelation 21:27 And there shall in no wise enter into it anything that defileth neither whatsoever worketh abomination, or maketh a lie, but they are written in the Lamb's book of life.

In Luke 10:20 we learn that the redeemed have their names written in heaven, *"Notwithstanding in this rejoice not, that the spirits are subject unto you; but rather rejoice because your names are written in heaven."*

In the Bible the name of Jesus is emphasized and the importance of His name is throughout Scripture, which the following verses highlight:

Revelation 19:13, *"And he was clothed with a vesture dipped in blood and his name is called the Word of God."*

Revelation 19:16, *"And he hath on his vesture and on his thigh a name written, King of Kings and Lord of Lords."*

In contrast let's look at the significance of a name. We see that at the name of Jesus every knee will bow and every tongue will confess. We see at the sealing of the 144 thousand the name of God is in their foreheads.

Revelation 3:12 tells us: *"He who overcomes I will make him a pillar in the Temple of My God, and he shall go out no more, and I will write on him the name of My God, and the name of the city of My God, the New Jerusalem, which comes down out of heaven from My God; and I will write on him My new name."*

In contrast we have the statement, *"Here is wisdom and let he who has understanding count the number of his name."* The wisdom is that those who are numbered are appointed to death and the reason the Antichrist has a number for his name is because from his birth he is destined for death because he is the son of Satan himself.

The other shocking reality is that if you do not have a name in heaven, you are essentially a number. Upon my first realization that my unsaved loved ones are mere numbers I felt the same horror that Charlton Heston felt in the movie "Soylent Green" when he realized that the food that Soylent Green was made from people.

The reason the Antichrist has a number for a name is because he is the son of Satan and is not only appointed to eternal death from his birth but will bodily be thrown into the lake of fire. It is important for the Tribulation Saint to fully understand that this man is the son of Satan. Those who number themselves with his number and take the number of his name will also be numbered for death. The Bible cannot seem to drive this point far enough that the man that is on the earth is the son of Satan himself. We see this driven home even further when we get to the next phrase.

IV. Solving the Revelation 13:18 Riddle : His number *is* 666.

The fact that this man is Satan is further reinforced by, "His number is 666."

The number six, translated from the New Testament Greek into English, means "vex," or "curse," because he who bears this number is cursed. To be cursed in the Bible means to be viewed with contempt, dishonor, insignificant, of little esteem, dishonored, vile, despised, abated, and erased.

Cursed means abhorred, detested, laid under a curse, rendering their days unfortunate. We see cursed in the Bible as destroying and bringing hardship. Not only is the man of sin cursed but he brings a curse onto the world by virtue of his identity.

A triple six is a triple curse both on him and on the world. Six in the Bible is the number of man and the fall brought on man the curse of God.

AS Seven represents God's number of perfection, six represents that which is below it that is one shy of seven. Was not Satan the highest angel, below God Himself. The triple is a trinity, which in the Bible is a number of completeness. A complete curse, the embodiment of all evil and the ultimate curse on mankind and now he walks and reigns among them.

The triple six also represents the unholy trinity, with the Devil acting as God. The Antichrist, whom Satanists call the son of Satan, mimics Jesus Christ. The False Prophet who the Bible predicts will comes onto the earth and performs miracles to get the masses to worship the Beast, mocks God's Holy Spirit. The unholy trinity are named in Scriptures as "The Dragon," "The Beast," and "The False Prophet." The Dragon is Satan in the Revelation, it means a great serpent.

A snake is a reptile, cold blooded, slimy, slithering, with a quick and stinging bite. A snake must rely on the sun to regulate its body temperature. They also do not blink. The king cobra the world's largest poisonous snake is strong enough to kill an elephant. In the Old Testament dragon also meant a large sea monster, dinosaur and crocodile. All are large, frightening, menacing and cold.

Thus the number 666 is synonymous with Satan himself and is the number of the Devil. One who is cursed, who brings a curse onto mankind and who is a number because he is ordained for eternal death from his birth. He will now directly challenge the followers of the living God and seek to annihilate them. If he cannot take them with him to eternal hell by numbering them along with himself, he will destroy their lives and murder them.

We see the martyrs crying to God from under the alter in Revelation 6:10, *"And they cried with a loud voice saying, How long O Lord holy and true , until you judge and avenge our blood on those who dwell on the earth."*

V. Solving the Revelation 13:18 Riddle : 666 is the Ultimate Idolatry

The number 666 has another meaning that signifies evil in the Bible. When we dig deeper into 666 in the Bible we uncover more clues to decoding the riddle and to the meaning of 666. We see 666 relating to idolatry. The sin of idolatry breaks the first and second commandments.

Adonikams came back from Babylon with 666 of his descendants and he was a high priest from Babylon and his name means my lord stands or rises and stands means like on a pedestal of gold.

When we think of golden images we cannot forget the golden calf that Aaron made in Exodus 32 from the golden earrings everyone wore and contributed.

In the book of Daniel, Nebuchadnezzar's idolatrous golden image was 60 cubits high by 6 cubits wide, thus 66. Here we see idolatry in the golden image. Daniel was thrown into the fiery furnace for not worshipping the image. We see a parallel in Revelation 13:15, *"He was granted power to give breath to the image of the beast, that the image of the beast should both speak and cause as many as would not worship the image of the beast to be killed."* Just like Nebuchadnezzar we see Antichrist set up his idolatrous image. The book of Daniel makes it very plain that the Antichrist will set himself up as a god. We see the number 666 linked with idolatry.

The tribe of Dan which is the tribe the Antichrist descends was given to idolatry. The Antichrist will have Jewish ancestry and will rise from the tribe of Dan, for more on the Antichrist see my book, *The Antichrist of Revelation:666*. Dan set up Micah's idol made of silver.

To understand the idolatry piece of the tribe of Dan we must first look to Rachel, Dan's mother who bore him through a surrogate or a concubine.

Rachel, the wife of Jacob was both beautiful and like most biblical patriarchs had her area of sin. Rachel could not have any children and became jealous of her sister Leah who bore Jacob four sons while she sat childless. She became angry at Jacob and blamed him for her childless state. In Rachel's jealousy she grabbed her maid Bilhah, and gave her to Jacob as a surrogate to have children for her, and Bilhah bore Dan. Jealous rivalry continued between Rachel and Leah. Rachel's maid bore a second son to her: Naphtali.

When Jacob left the home of his father in law, Rachel stole his idols and lied to her father as he searched for them so that he would not find them. She also kept this secret from her husband Jacob who did not know that she had stolen the idols from her father. Rachel's attachment to the idols was so great that she stole them and lied to protect them. No doubt she was thrilled over the birth of Dan and doted over him and he followed her in the area of her idolatry.

Judges Chapters 17 and 18 tells the story of Micah an idolater who lived in the mountains of Ephraim and who employed a renegade, idolatrous priest. Dan and 600 of his men went searching the land for an area to settle in and came upon Micah's house. They forcibly took his idols and his priest to serve them. They then went into Laish took the land by murdering its inhabitants, renamed it Dan and set up Micah's idol and employed idolatrous priests to serve them until their captivity.

Dan set up idolatry in defiance of Israel's God. King Jeroboam, Israel's northern kingdom's first king who the Bible mentions over and over as *"the man who caused Israel to sin"* placed two golden calves, which he set up for idolatrous worship. He placed one in Bethel and the other in Dan, which both lay on the extreme southern and northern part of the kingdom. (I Kings 29-30) Bethel afterwards became a center for Idolatry. Dan already existed as one, which is why Jeroboam placed a calf there. Amos foretells Israel's captivity, in Amos 8:14 God's declares judgment on Dan for its allegiance to its false gods.

The Bible well establishes the idolatry of the tribe of Dan. This is one reason it is not mentioned among the 12 tribes in Revelation chapter 7 and is the lineage of the Antichrist. The Antichrist sets himself up as a god via his cloned avatar in the Third Temple, which he causes the world to worship and commits the ultimate idolatry and abomination. We see idolatry in the Antichrist's lineage, to his demand for worship of his idolatrous image to his claiming to be God. All through the Bible we see 666 associated with idolatry. The Bible tells us that demons are in the idols and with idolatry comes a curse. See Deuteronomy 32:16-17, 1 Corinthians 10:20, Deuteronomy 27:15.

VI. Solving the Revelation 13:18 Riddle: the Beast, Idolatry Currency and Gold

In Scripture currency is synonymous with idolatry. The image of Micah was made from money that the mother of a boy saved for the purpose of making it into an idol which ended up in Micah's home. Dan set up Micah's idol which was made from 1100 shekels of silver (we see currency as idolatry) So now we begin to see that idolatry as it relates to 666 is linked with currency. This is very clear in Chronicles 9:13. The Bible tells us that after the Queen of Sheba's visit, Solomon yearly took in 666 talents of gold from the surrounding nations. Deuteronomy 17:15-17 warns that a king of Israel shall not multiply wives, silver or gold which Solomon did in addition to going after the gods of his foreign wives and building high places for them. 1 Kings Chapter 11 describes Solomon's descent into idolatry. Solomon's 666 talents of gold was both currency and related to his own idolatry. We see 666 as relating to both idolatry and gold, which is currency.

Throughout history, ancient and modern nations use gold for currency. Only after World War II did the world stop using gold as a reserve for currencies. Gold, that is money is synonymous with idolatry.

In James Rickard's book, *The Death of Money: The Collapse of the International Monetary System*, which is one of the best books on the coming dollar collapse you can read, James Rickards spends a good deal of time in his book talking about gold and the importance of gold in the international monetary system. He stated that while there is no official gold standard it is very important in finance and the standard still exists though not formally. He also points out that the euro has more gold reserves than the US. The golden head, the golden image relates to 666 and to currency as gold reserves back currency.

We see gold and silver as currency in the description of the Prince of Tyre, who is compared to the Antichrist, Ezekiel 28:4-5 states, *"You have gained riches for yourself, and gathered gold and silver into your treasuries, by your wisdom in trade you have increased your riches and your heart is lifted up because of your riches."*

Nebuchadnezzar was depicted as the head of fine gold. Daniel 2:32-33 describes, *"The image's head was of fine gold, its chest and arms of silver, its belly and thighs of bronze, its feet partly of iron and partly of clay."* Daniel tells Nebuchadnezzar in verse 37, *"You are this head of gold."* The Bible tells us that the reason it had a head of gold was because of its power, strength and glory and wealth. In the Antichrist's image we can expect to see a correlation of gold with currency.

There is also the pattern established in the Bible that the currency buys the idol or the currency is turned into the idol. In Exodus God commands the children of Israel not to make an idol of gold or silver. Exodus 20:23 states: *"Ye shall not make with me gods of silver, neither shall ye make unto you gods of gold."*

After all of these instructions, Moses goes up to the mountain with God and while he was gone a while the children of Israel got bored and discouraged and had Aaron make them a golden calf.

Exodus 32:31 states, *"And Moses returned unto the Lord, and said, Oh, this people have sinned a great sin, and have made them gods of gold."*

The image of the Beast is made during the Antichrist's reign after he survives his fatal wound. Most likely his government will commission a considerable amount of money to have the image made and to have it made quickly.

We get the impression from Revelation 13 that the survival from the fatal wound is remarkable and the False Prophet uses it to justify the commissioning of the image.

Revelation 13:14 affirms, *"And deceiveth them that dwell on the earth by the means of those miracles which he had power to do in the sight of the beast; saying to them that dwell on the earth, that they should make an image to the beast, which had the wound by a sword, and did live."*

With the image of the Beast and the mark of the Beast and the technology that helps it come into being along with the money that is used to fund it, we see the fulfillment of Daniel 11:38:

"But in his estate shall he honor the God of forces: and a god whom his fathers knew not shall he honor with gold, and silver, and with precious stones, and pleasant things."

VII. Numerology of Gold Represents the Heavenly or Idolatry

Gold in the Bible is a dichotomy, it represents idolatry but also represents the heavens.

Numerology-the Heavenly

We see Solomon in 1Kings Chapter 6 Solomon making the temple of pure gold, including the floor. 1 Kings 6:30 states, *"And the floor of the house he overlaid with gold, within and without."* We then see the gold and silver given as an offering for the building of the arc of the covenant which was made from pure gold and for the lampstands and bowls used in the worship of God. We see gold used in the priests clothing as well.

Exodus 28:36 commands, *"And thou shalt make a plate of pure gold, and grave upon it, like the engravings of a signet, HOLINESS TO THE LORD."*

When we think of the description of heaven we think of streets of gold. In the book of Revelation we are told in Revelation 21:18 that the Holy City is made of pure gold like clear glass. Revelation 21:21 specifies that the streets are made of pure gold like transparent glass. There are four uses for gold in the Bible:

1. Representing the heavenly
2. Representing idolatry
3. For currency to buy and sell
4. For ornamentation-jewelry

In the verses for gold's heavenly uses we see the number 12, which is also the number of the apostles and the 12 tribes of Israel. Note the following verses:

Numbers 7: 84: *"This was the dedication of the alter, in the day when it was anointed, by the princes of Israel: twelve chargers of silver, twelve silver bowls, <u>twelve spoons of gold</u>."*

Numbers 7: 86: *"The <u>golden spoons were twelve</u>, full of incense, weighing ten shekels a piece, after the shekel of the sanctuary: all <u>the gold of the spoons was an hundred and twenty</u> shekels."*

The total of 120 shekels is our number 12 again.

We see the Queen of Sheba giving 120 talents of gold to Solomon. 2 Chronicles 9:9 affirms, *"And she gave the king <u>an hundred and twenty talents of gold</u>, and of spices great abundance, and precious stones: neither was there any such spice as the Queen of Sheba gave king Solomon."*

In Revelation 21 in the depiction of the New Jerusalem we see the number 12 throughout in the measurements of the Holy City, where God Himself will dwell among His people.

Numerology on the evil side:

Notice in the previous passages the number 12 and the number 12 for the alter, but Micah's idol was 11, which is one short of 12 as six is one short of seven. Notice also the 66 cubits of Nebuchadnezzar's image. Daniel 3:1 describes the idolatrous image, *"Nebuchadnezzar the king made an image of gold whose height was 60 cubits, and the breadth there of six cubits: he set it up in the plain of Dura, in the province of Babylon."*

As with the graven images in the Old Testament, we are told in Revelation 13: 14 (the False Prophet) says to them that dwell on the earth, that they should make an image to the Beast, and the riddle with the number 666 follows in Revelation 13:18 as the number of the name of the Beast.

We see 666 associated with idolatry. Solomon took in 666 shekels of gold a year. Solomon was given to idolatry. He violated Deuteronomy 17:17, which commanded: *"Neither shall he multiply wives to himself, that his heart turn not away: neither shall he greatly multiply to himself silver and gold."*

Ezekiel's vision in the sixth year in the sixth month is one of great abominations of idolatry taking place within the Jewish temple.

Thus we have idolatry represented as six, and we see double sixes and ultimately the triple six in the Revelation, which is the idolatry that leads to the end of the age.

Gold on any idol was corrupt and an abomination to God

The very gold used on the idols or graven images itself is an abomination to God that he says to discard as a monstrous cloth. Deuteronomy 7:25 states, *"The carved images of their gods shall ye burn with fire: though shalt not desire the silver or gold that is on them, nor take it unto thee, lest though be snared therein: for it is an abomination to the LORD thy God."*

Isaiah 30:22 adds, *" Ye shall defile also the covering of thy graven images of silver, and the ornament of thy molten images of gold: thou shalt cast them away as a monstrous cloth; thou shalt say unto it, Get thee hence."*

When God gave the Israelites victory over Jericho, He commanded the Israelites not to bring out of the City any of the accursed items. Achan disobeyed and took out various items including gold. Achan's sin of taking the Babylonian garment and a wedge of gold and two hundred shekels of silver after caused God to withdraw from Israel and they fell to a weak enemy (Ai A-I) until the sin was found out and Achan and his family were destroyed. God's anger then subsided (Joshua 7.)

Joshua 6: 18 states, *"And you, by all means abstain from the accursed things, lest you become accursed when you take of the accursed things , and make the camp of Israel a curse, and trouble it."*

The very gold that is used on an idol becomes an abomination to God and a curse to the partaker and was to be discarded.
Thus we see the curse associated with idolatry and more so of the idolatry associated with the triple six of Revelation 13:18.

10
The Mark of the Beast Meets Geopolitics

While many writers will talk about the mark of the Beast and how the Antichrist will institute it, a key piece is that he must be in a political position to fulfill what the Scriptures predict. Before we go any further in this report I want to show you what is equally as hair-raising as the technologies that are available to fulfill the mark of the Beast, is that the leading position in the European Union, which is the final world empire that will launch the Antichrist will allow him access to these technologies and the ability to implement them. See my book: *The Seat of the Antichrist Bible Prophecy and the European Union* for the report on how without a doubt the EU is the final world empire.

The European Commission president leads the European Union and in my book I have identified it as the Seat of the Antichrist because it would allow the Antichrist all of the powers outlined in Scripture.

Concerning the mark of the Beast technology the way that the EU is structured would allow the Antichrist direct access to the latest technologies and the ability to implement them EU and then worldwide. Technological advances are important to the EU's economic growth and prosperity.

The Commission presidency has a team of commissioners that it appoints who report to the president. One of them is the Commissioner for Research, Science and Innovation. There is the possibility that at the time of the Antichrist, this role can be filled by the False Prophet. I previously leaned in the direction of the False Prophet being a religious leader, but during the research for this report I saw the similarities of religious and scientific beliefs. The book of Daniel indirectly refers to technology as a false god. It is very likely that the False Prophet can be a scientist who advocates for the Antichrist and technology.

Today science is a Tower of Babel with scientists believing that they can be like God by perfecting his creation and achieve immortality and defeat aging. The False Prophet will advocate this as well, but will mainly promote the Antichrist.

The European Union's Commissioners for Science and Research's reports to the Commission president, which in the future will be the Antichrist and his responsibilities are as follows:

Making sure that research funding programs, notably Horizon 2020, contribute to the Commission's jobs, growth and investment package.

Horizon 2020 promises breakthroughs, discoveries and world firsts because it provides the funding for scientists. It has allocated a whopping 80 billion euros available until 2020 to help fund these discoveries.

Scientists submit a proposal for their research project and it is evaluated by the Commission, if the Commission likes the project it draws up a grant agreement with the participant. The European Commission then draws up a grant agreement with each participant. The grant agreement confirms what research & innovation activities will be undertaken, the project duration, budget, rates and costs, European Commission's contribution, all rights and obligations and more.

The Commissioner for Science and Research oversees Horizon 2020 to make sure the selected projects lead to the EU's economic growth. He also promotes the international excellence of the EU's research and science and he helps strengthen research capacities and innovation across all Member States. In addition the Commissioner evaluates how EU-funded research can be used more effectively. He ensures that Commission proposals are based on scientific evidence.

According to the Commission's own wording, " He also encourages private companies to apply research to meet challenges faced by society and create more high-quality jobs. " This means that under the Antichrist he will have the ability to influence the "Mark of the Beast" technology.

The Commission also states of the duties of the Commissioner:

"The Commissioner is also responsible for establishing strong coordination across the Commission regarding research, science and innovation matters, to make sure that Commission proposals and activities are based on sound scientific evidence and contribute best to jobs and growth agenda. He is supported by a Directorate-General for Research and Innovation (RTD) and he or she reports to the Commissioner for Research, Science and Innovation."

In addition to the Commissioner for Science and Research's role, The Joint Research Centre, under the responsibility of Commissioner for Education, Culture, Youth and Sport, is the European Commission's science service.

Its mission is to support EU policies and the JRC provides independent scientific and technical advice to the European Commission to support a wide range of European Union policies, and it will also assist in the 'Mark of the Beast' technology and its implementation.

The JRC also maximizes the value of Horizon 2020, which is the biggest EU Research and Innovation program ever that promises more breakthroughs, discoveries and world-firsts by taking great ideas from the lab to the market.

The groundwork is already laid for the implementation of the Mark of the Beast through the current EU institutional structure and even with further changes in those bodies as the EU moves towards political union this structure should not change. It is noteworthy that it already exists without further evolution of the EU. The fact that this infrastructure is already in place as the technologies that fit the image of the beast and mark of the Beast are appearing shows how close we are to the start of the Tribulation.

11

The Seed of Satan & Immortality-Garden of Eden's DNA Changing Trees

In 1990, the Human Genome Project, an international scientific research initiative with the aim of mapping all of the genes of the human genome, was formally launched and in this environment, led to advances in DNA sequencing, which is the process of determining the precise order of nucleotides within a DNA molecule.

In 2012 Jennifer Doudna discovered essentially how to edit genomic DNA, via her discovery of CRISPR Cas9, which is a protein found in Streptococcus bacteria that works like a scissors. The protein attacks its prey, the DNA of viruses and slices it up. Thus came the ability to genetically engineer DNA by editing it. Scientists can delete or insert specific bits of DNA into cells with incredible precision.

This genome editing discovery allowed scientists to create glow bunnies by taking the DNA of glow jellyfish and inserting it into the DNA of rabbits. It launched the idea of designer babies, curing disease, and improving on creation. Some scientists inserted spider DNA into goat embryos and the goat's milk produced silk and they created bullet proof human skin.

Evangelical Christians have theorized that the Mark of the Beast can be a DNA change that all must take and the DNA alteration will make humans unhuman. They have concluded that this would be the first time that DNA would be transformed by Satan via scientists, which adds to its horror. This is incorrect, the first DNA change occurred in the garden of Eden.

In the garden were two trees, the tree of knowledge of good and evil, which Adam and Eve were not allowed to eat it's fruit and the tree of life, from which they could eat and it would cause them to live forever.

I. The DNA Changing Tree of the Knowledge of Good and Evil Vs. Tree of Life

Man was created to live alongside God and initially man lived in Paradise, which is the Garden of Eden. Man could have eaten of the tree of life, but the one tree he was forbidden from eating was the tree that would cause him both physical and spiritual death. This is why the tree is called the tree of knowledge of good and evil because man at this time only knew good and he did not understand evil, but once he ate of the apple, he knew evil and what was good and evil. When the garden is first described we see the tree of life and by it was the tree of the knowledge of good and evil. In the garden man was free to choose, he could choose life or he could choose evil.

The tree was an actual tree, a super tree, similar in power to the tree of life. Its fruit has the ability to change human DNA. The tree of life will change our mortal bodies to eternal and transform every cell in our body and supercharge it via a DNA change. Meanwhile the tree of the knowledge of good and evil had the ability to take a human body that would not age and cause it to age and die. In bringing this corruption to the physical body it also wrought corruption in the soul and heart of man.

Then the serpent said to the woman, "You will not surely die."(Genesis 3:4) The Devil knew that the woman would not die instantly but she would now experience both spiritual and physical death. The devil came and tempted Eve into eating the tree, he wanted her to eat of it. He lied to Eve and said, *"For God knows that in the day you eat of it your eyes will be opened, and you will be like God knowing good and evil."* At this time Eve did not know what evil was or that it existed. The Devil made it sound to Eve as if knowing the good and the evil was something God was keeping from her. Thinking that the fruit would make her wise she ate of it and gave it to Adam and both of their eyes were opened. This fruit had the power to change the entire body chemistry. The evil she would come to have knowledge of she would wish she had never known.

She would eat the fruit and her DNA changed, and she would have Adam eat of it and his DNA changed. Romans 5:12 tells us what happened when Adam sinned and how death came to everyone because of Adam's sin. It states, *"Therefore, just as through one man sin entered the world, and death through sin, and thus death spread to all men, because all sinned."*

God cursed both man and woman and the serpent. First he cursed the serpent, and said that He would put enmity between her seed and his seed in Genesis 3:15: *"And I will put enmity between you and the woman, And between your seed and her Seed, He shall bruise your head And you shall bruise His heel."*

The Devil won a victory in the garden by bringing sin and death into the world and by so doing, he would have offspring. He would now acquire the souls of men, but God let him know that this would be for Him a battle of the ages, for from the woman who he deceived and tempted would come the deliver and Savior who would reconcile man to God who would crush Satan in the end.

To the woman he gives her pain in childbirth, prior to eating the apple she would not have experienced pain in childbirth, this means that the uterus as a muscle would not constrict so painfully to deliver, as all of the pain in childbirth comes from the uterus which is a muscle constricting to push the baby out. This muscle must have been more flexible.

In addition, God said that a woman's sorrow will be increased and her desire will be to her husband. The emotions of women are exacerbated by hormones and they fluctuate. These were probably more regulated prior to the eating of the apple but the apple affected the various body systems of a woman and especially her hormones.

God also cursed man and the ground that he tilled. Prior to his eating the apple the earth was a bounty ripe for the picking, but now the earth would bring forth thorns and weeds and man will have to work hard for his bread, *"by the sweat of your brow."* In addition man would now experience the physical death of his body for he was cursed, *"till you return to the ground, for out of it you were taken, for dust you are, And to dust you shall return"* (Genesis 3:19). This was not God's first intention. Death became part of the curse on man and in line with Satan's plan. He does not tell man and you will die and be gone forever, You shall return to dust and be no more, but *'to dust you shall return.'*

God's original intention was that man would eat of the tree of life and live forever and not return to dust. His returning to dust would put his body in a state of what the Bible calls sleep until the judgement day.

In death though the spirit departs, it is like a battery in a battery terminal and the battery is specific to that terminal. There is something that remains even in the dust of a human being to recreate the DNA for the bodies that come after our death, which from our original bodies there is something that remains even in the dust of a human being to recreate the DNA for the spiritual bodies promised after our death. Our spirits are somehow connected to our bodies on a cellular level. Those persons who have accepted Jesus Christ as their personal Savior will go onto eternal life and eating of the tree of life while those who refuse Him will go into the lake of fire for eternity. It should be noted that the lake of fire does not completely destroy the glorified bodies as it would a human body, but causes great torment.

The tree of the knowledge of good and evil and the tree of life are DNA changing trees. These trees offer supercharged fruit. The tree of the knowledge of good and evil contained a protein or its own version of CRISPR cas9 to alter the DNA of Adam and Eve. The tree of life on the other hand changes human DNA so that the body will not die and it is not reversible meaning that the DNA cannot be penetrated and cut by a CRISPR cas 9 type of protein. We know its effects on the DNA are not reversible or God would not have hid and guarded the tree to keep man from eating its fruit.

II. The DNA Changing Tree of the Knowledge of Good and Evil

The tree of the knowledge of good and evil brought in disease and death and is the opposite of the tree of life in that it corrupted the original DNA and design of man. In addition to bringing in disease and physical death, we see a change in the woman's birth process as going from painless to very painful and a change in the muscles and body for the muscle to feel pain.

In addition to the physical detonation came the knowledge of good and evil meaning that emotionally and spiritually came a spiritual deterioration. The best way to compare it is to an active alcoholic or a drug addict who go from being upstanding members of communities to lying stealing criminals in pursuit of their drug. Or alcoholics who grow mean, angry and resentful as alcohol changes their emotions and brain chemistry and brings out base emotions.

The knowledge of good and evil was not a good thing because prior to the genetic change, man and woman were in a higher state of mind and could not have comprehended evil the way that an honest person cannot comprehend a pathological liar, or a gentle person can comprehend a sadistic murderer.

After Adam and Eve ate the apple we see them immediately feeling shame and the evidence of this is they sewed fig leaves to cover themselves. Adam also hides from God. When God asks Adam if he ate of the tree he told him not to eat from he immediately blames Eve and does not take responsibility for his own actions and attempts to deceive God.

The tree of knowledge of good and evil's fruit was so toxic to the body that God commanded Adam and Eve to not even touch it.

Genesis 3:3 records, *"But of the fruit of the tree which is in the midst of the garden, God has said, You shall not eat it, nor shall you touch it, lest you die."*

What should be noted is the scientific truth taught in this verse that the skin absorbs, a common delivery method of pain medicine is through skin patches, and that is just one example.

III. The Seed of Satan-the change of Man's DNA

In the condemnation of the Devil for tempting Eve, God said to Satan in Genesis 3:15:

"And I will put enmity between you and the woman, and between your seed and her seed; he shall bruise your head, and you shall bruise his heel."

The seed of Satan was in the fruit from the tree of the knowledge of good and evil. Satan or Lucifer was a covering cherub in the Garden of Eden. He was the most powerful and beautiful angel. With his presence in Eden he knew the garden well.

We do not know why the tree was in the garden to begin with or why it was used, but its effect was so negative on the DNA of man and woman that God regarded it as the seed of Satan.

In John 8:42-44, Jesus refers to the unbeliever as being of their father the devil:

[42] *Jesus said to them, "If God were your Father, you would love Me, for I proceeded forth and came from God; nor have I come of Myself, but He sent Me.*
[43] *Why do you not understand My speech? Because you are not able to listen to My word.*
[44] *You are of your father the devil, and the desires of your father you want to do. He was a murderer from the beginning, and does not stand in the truth, because there is no truth in him. When he speaks a lie, he speaks from his own resources, for he is a liar and the father of it. (Acts 13;10, 1John3:8.)*

IV. The serpent in the garden-A Satan possessed snake

In the garden account the idea of a serpent speaking to Eve sounds unbelievable but we learn in the Bible that demon spirits enter into humans and we read in the Bible in one case they went into pigs, so we know demons can enter into living beings. How else was Satan to appear to the woman but to inhabit a living creature and he chose the serpent.

In the Revelation Satan is referred to as the Dragon. The garden was a unique place where no other humans inhabited except for Adam and Eve who God created so Satan's only alternative was to inhabit a non-human living creature. Notice that the woman had no fear of the snake and this was because she was in her pre DNA changed state and didn't feel fear until after they ate the fruit.

The tree of the life gives man's body eternal life. In the garden Adam existed with God in the same state that we will exist once we die and get our resurrected body's. But, when Adam ate of the forbidden tree he made his body corruptible and it became corrupt with sin. This sin gave him a knowledge into evil that he did not have before because now he was corrupt and defiled. Horror of horrors once man ate of the tree of knowledge of good and evil, God did not want him to eat of the tree of life because that would have made his sinful self an eternal being who would never die the death that he must die. It would have reprogrammed the DNA so that he would live forever but in a corrupted state.

Since the DNA of man and woman was changed and their father was now the devil, there would need to be a new birth in Christ, with his sacrifice for our sins, to redeem us from death.

Genesis 3:22 Then the Lord God said, behold the man has become like one of Us, to know good and evil. And now lest he put out his hand and also take of the tree of life, and eat and live forever. Satan changed the DNA of humans and imparted his seed via the fruit of the tree that Adam and Eve ate.

V. When Seed of Satan Changed Man's DNA Angel of Death and Hades Appeared

Once man's DNA changed after Eve ate from the DNA changing tree of the knowledge of good and evil and Satan became man's father by imparting his seed into man via this DNA change, he would die and go to Satan his father after his death without redemption. Adam and Eve's eating of the fruit empowered two principalities and powers of Satan. Paul in Ephesians 6:12 writes *For we wrestle not against flesh and blood, but against principalities, against powers, against the rulers of the darkness of this world, against spiritual wickedness in high places.*

Two of those principalities are mentioned in the Revelation because they both were given their task when Adam and Eve ate the fruit and they are Death and Hades.

Death is not figurative in the Revelation, Death is a principality and he came into the garden at the moment of the DNA change, when the seed of Satan changed man and woman's DNA and they would now die and Death would assist in bringing the souls, the sons and daughters of Satan to Hades. In Revelation 6:8 we are told that Hades follows Death. In Revelation 20:13-14 we see them mentioned two more times and again they are together. The verse states:

[13] The sea gave up the dead who were in it, and Death and Hades delivered up the dead who were in them. And they were judged, each one according to his works. [14] Then Death and Hades were cast into the lake of fire. This is the second death.

Death and Hades are referred to as them substantiating that they are individual Demons and they are both cast into the lake of fire.

Death in all its morbidity and sorrow was never what God intended. He intended for everyone to live in Eden the Paradise of God, never knowing evil and walking in fellowship with Him. The fruit of the tree of good and evil defiled man and brought him under the reign of Satan. As Jesus is the Bread of Life, that sustains the believer this fruit which was pleasant to the eyes and good for food in contrast to the bread of life and fountains of living waters brought in corruption, sin and death. The tree was cursed, when Adam and Eve partook of its fruit, they cursed mankind. A tree, which cursed man with sin, Jesus would hang on and his death would redeem man from the curse of the tree. Galatians 3:13 states, *"cursed is everyone who hangs on a tree."*

Trees in the Bible represent people, we see this with Nebuchadnezzar and his vision of the tree, which the prophet Daniel told him represented him. Trees without their leaves resemble arteries and veins. The tree of life is a representation of Christ and his veins and arteries that bled out and provides life for all who believe. With the tree a symbol for life, cursed became anyone who hung on a tree in death because the depiction of a man dead on a tree, which is a symbol of life is a symbol of eternal damnation, which is why Jesus depicted as hanging on a tree, is a symbol of his death being the substitute for our sins.

Regarding the mark of the Beast being a DNA change to be like the Antichrist or like Satan, man already has the seed of Satan and only by a second birth in Christ Jesus can he be redeemed from the curse of sin.

VI. The Tree of Life Supercharges Man's DNA to immortality

The tree of the life gives man's body eternal life. In the garden Adam existed with God in a body that was not prone to sickness, death or base emotions. But, when Adam ate of the forbidden tree he made his body corruptible and it became corrupt with sin. This sin gave him knowledge into evil that he did not have before because now he was corrupt and defiled. Horror of horrors once man ate of the tree of knowledge of good and evil, God did not want him to eat of the tree of life because that would have made his sinful self an eternal being who would never die the death that he must die. It would have reprogrammed the DNA so that he would live forever but in a corrupted state. In the Revelation the tree of life is elaborated on and Jesus promises believers that they will eat the fruit of the tree.

The book of Revelation states that the tree of life bears 12 kinds of fruit and its leaves contain healing properties. We also see that in the afterlife those who are of Christ will be granted to eat of the tree and we also see that Adam and Eve were granted as well, but once they ate of the tree of the knowledge of good and evil the tree of life was hidden from them.

Genesis 3:22-24: *Then the LORD God said, "Behold, the man has become like one of Us, knowing good and evil; and now, he might stretch out his hand, and take also from the tree of life, and eat, and live forever"-- therefore the LORD God sent him out from the garden of Eden, to cultivate the ground from which he was taken. So He drove the man out; and at the east of the garden of Eden He stationed the cherubim and the flaming sword, which turned every direction to guard the way to the tree of life."*

Revelation 22:1-2: *Then he showed me a river of the water of life, clear as crystal, coming from the throne of God and of the Lamb, in the middle of its street On either side of the river was the tree of life, bearing twelve kinds of fruit, yielding its fruit every month; and the leaves of the tree were for the healing of the nations.*

Revelation 2:7: *He who has an ear, let him hear what the Spirit says to the churches To him who overcomes, I will grant to eat of the tree of life which is in the Paradise of God.'*

Revelation 22:14-15: *Blessed are those who wash their robes, so that they may have the right to the tree of life, and may enter by the gates into the city. Outside are the dogs and the sorcerers and the immoral persons and the murderers and the idolaters, and everyone who loves and practices lying.*

The tree of life is the tree of immortality, it is the super fruit of super fruit and it has the power to alter human DNA and eradicate disease from the genes and render the human body an eternal vessel. It supercharges human DNA from mortal to immortal. All believers will eat of it because this is what Jesus promised.

Satan already changed the DNA of humans and imparted his seed via the fruit of the tree that Adam and Eve ate. So then why would another DNA change be on Satan's agenda, it is not a direction that the science is moving with human engineering, not for a police state. What is happening in the scientific fields dealing with DNA is the Tower of Babel mentality. Man believes that by altering DNA he can act like God and attempt to make changes in the human race. Should we be surprised that this is an area that Satan would go?

VII. Gold and DNA-Its Relation Revealed in the Garden of Eden

The word gold is used 417 times in the Bible. We see it first used in Genesis mentioned as the first River of the parted four riverheads that flow from the River in the Garden of Eden named Pison and it *"skirts the whole land of Havilah where there is gold."* (Genesis. 2:11) The name Pison itself means increase. We see from this verse that Eden bordered a land rich in gold. What is noteworthy about this is that gold has an affinity with DNA and scientists are using gold nanoparticles from strengthening it when combined with the particles it aids in diagnostics as well as a building block for nanotechnology. Gold nanoparticles also unravel DNA's double helix. It is then no coincidence that we see a land rich in gold mentioned as surrounding Eden with its two DNA changing trees: the tree of the knowledge of good and evil and the tree of life.

Scientists think that gold exists within asteroids and meteorites and might have even been brought to earth via meteor showers, which adds even more interest to the metal.

VIII. Is The Mark of the Beast A DNA Change?

What we know thus far is the Antichrist will have the means to the latest technology and that an avatar, android, humanoid fits the image of the beast and the philosophy that goes with it, that the Antichrist is now immortal and man has achieved immortality. People will worship him for this and we know that he will use a good deal of money to make his cloned image. I have established that the mark is not a DNA change. There is the possibility that the image of the Beast can be connected to the mark of the Beast.

In the area of DNA change and a DNA change as part of the mark of the Beast, possibly but not in the way evangelicals are expecting, which is that we will receive a DNA change that will not make us fully human and we will be part beast or machine. Considering that Satan already orchestrated the first DNA change in the garden and that we know we have his seed, it is more in line that Satan would get scientists to believe they can achieve immortality in this imperfect body that he corrupted and this is accomplished in his image, which will receive part of his consciousness because he will still exist in his human body. It also is demonic to use DNA to change creation that are already being tested. It is possible that Antichrist will condone DNA testing that changes creation and will allow bazaar and demonic tests performed on the human body.

Just as Joseph Mengella conducted gross experiments for Adolph Hitler, men and women will be used as human Guinee pigs for the DNA cutting and splicing. As of right now there are no experiments that would fit the Mark of the Beast as a DNA change for the human race. This is not to say that a DNA nanobot or something related to DNA cannot be a part, but not in the area of splicing our current DNA. There just is no evidence of that in the current science field today nor is that the area that science is moving forward. Scientists are looking to perfect the human body and give it super human capabilities, eradicate disease, reverse aging and make men immortal. But, DNA splicing and experiments will most likely occur in the Antichrist's police state.

12

Technology that fits the Mark of the Beast

It is my thought that the Antichrist will be connected to his followers just as Jesus is connected to His through the Holy Spirit. In my book *The Seat of the Antichrist,* I made mention of a quote from a scientist of what was next on the horizon in technological advances and since then the particular technology sited has made great strides. It is called brain interface and it allows one to think a thought and cause an action in a computer. It has been used so far for medical reasons, such as with use of a robotic limb that the person can think a thought and cause to move. At first it required being hooked up to a helmet full of electrodes but now it only requires an implantable device and I even read of a device that does not have to be implanted and can rest on the outer brain.

The technology even connected two brains, a human and a rat and a man was able to wave the tail of a rat. According to Future Tense "Its like they're reading my mind, how next generation apps will market your brainwaves:

In the last few years, the cost of EEG devices has dropped considerably, and consumer-grade headsets are becoming more affordable and can now be purchased for as little as $100. Companies are looking to these devices to produce:

Games, self-monitoring tools, touch free keyboards, vehicles that can detect driver drowsiness, lie detection, health insurance companies to give you rates based on your stress levels, and marketers gauging if you're hungry to show you ads for restaurants or select music playlists according to your mood.

A company has also come out with a phone that you do not have to speak into, you wear a collar around your neck and think and it picks up the vibrations and converts them to sound.

According to the EU which is where the Mark will originate and which holds the political seat of the Antichrist:

Computer scientists have predicted that within the next twenty years neural interfaces will be designed that will not only increase the dynamic range of senses, but will also enhance memory and enable "cyber think" — invisible communication with others.

This is only the tip of the iceberg, The international human genome project was launched in 1990 and completed in 2003 and resulted in the scientific strides we are seeing regarding DNA. Its counter was launched in 2013 by the European Commission and named the Human Brain Project, a European Commission future and emerging technologies flagship, it allows researchers across the globe to advance knowledge in the fields of neuroscience, computing, and brain-related medicine. In that same year the United States launched the Human Brain Initiative and hopes to achieve the same strides and discoveries as resulted from the Human Genome Project. The EU's Brain Project is funded for ten years and the US's provides for 12.

In the brain projects scientists are studying every neuron in the human brain, which functions like a highly advanced and sophisticated computer, to decipher the brain. Neuroscientist Randal Koene is planning to upload his brain to a computer. Koene plans to do so by mapping the brain, reducing its activity to computations and reproducing those computations in code. He believes this will allow humans to live indefinitely.

A scientist has already hooked up two men and had one man move the hand of the other man, initially this experiment started with a man wagging a rat's tail. Although this experiment was restricted to movement and not any other types of actions.

It gets even scarier than this, DARPA, the US intelligence agency known for emerging technologies and high tech surveillance, are developing synthetic telepathy so that soldiers can communicate via their thoughts and inserting chips in soldier's brains.

I. You'll have a choice between a brain or a hand chip

Revelation 13:16 states, *"He causes all, both small and great, rich and poor, free and slave, to receive a mark in their right hand or on their foreheads."*

What the Bible is telling us here is that the recipient of the mark will have a choice between having the chip in their hand or their forehead. There are two possibilities here:

1. The same mark will work from both locations and be the same technology that can go in either location on the body.

2. Or there will be two separate technologies that complete the same task.

On the implantable devices the suggested uses for them are endless. Other potential uses of implantable ICT devices include:

The human body as a medium for transmission of data (and energy) to "other devices such as cell phones and medical devices.

Location of persons and logging onto a website to find a family member.

Smart guns activated by the owner via their chip

Starting your automobile, opening your front door, via the chip. Paying for goods and services. Connecting to your computer.

Communicating your medical condition such as heart rate.

But, the mark of the Beast is going to be even more than just a payment system. You will be connected to the Antichrist's mainframe computer.

Currently the brain chip only works close to the brain, but the RFID chip, or two way NFC chip or Bluetooth low energy can be placed anywhere meaning in both places. I have seen RFIC chips go in the left hand and upper arm, but at the time of the Antichrist, they will be placed in the right hand or the forehead. Science is perfecting their technologies and ways of implementation and there is neural dust and ways being tested via nanotechnology, Now there are radio frequency tattoos that can be placed and serve the same function as an inserted chip.

II. Radio Frequency Tattoo Eerily Fits Mark of the Beast's Description

The mark may end up being one of these tattoos and the tattoos can be invisible.

This tattoo eerily mirrors Ezekiel 9:1-11, and counterfeits Christs action in the passage. The passage reads as follows:

Then He called out in my hearing with a loud voice, saying, "Let those who have charge over the city draw near, each with a deadly weapon in his hand." ² And suddenly six men came from the direction of the upper gate, which faces north, each with his battle-ax in his hand. One man among them was clothed with linen and had a writer's inkhorn at his side. They went in and stood beside the bronze altar.
³ Now the glory of the God of Israel had gone up from the cherub, where it had been, to the threshold of the temple.[a] And He called to the man clothed with linen, who had the writer's inkhorn at his side; ⁴ and the LORD said to him, "Go through the midst of the city, through the midst of Jerusalem, and put a mark on

the foreheads of the men who sigh and cry over all the abominations that are done within it."
⁵To the others He said in my hearing, "Go after him through the city and kill; do not let your eye spare, nor have any pity. ⁶Utterly slay old and young men, maidens and little children and women; but do not come near anyone on whom is the mark; and begin at My sanctuary." So they began with the elders who were before the temple.
⁷Then He said to them, "Defile the temple, and fill the courts with the slain. Go out!" And they went out and killed in the city. ⁸So it was, that while they were killing them, I was left alone; and I fell on my face and cried out, and said, "Ah, Lord GOD! Will You destroy all the remnant of Israel in pouring out Your fury on Jerusalem?"
⁹Then He said to me, "The iniquity of the house of Israel and Judah is exceedingly great, and the land is full of bloodshed, and the city full of perversity; for they say, 'The LORD has forsaken the land, and the LORD does not see!' ¹⁰And as for Me also, My eye will neither spare, nor will I have pity, but I will recompense their deeds on their own head."
¹¹Just then, the man clothed with linen, who had the inkhorn at his side, reported back and said, "I have done as You commanded me."

The man clothed in linen with the inkhorn in this passage is none other than Jesus Christ. During the middle of the Tribulation, the Antichrist is the one with the inkhorn, it is his counterpart to the spiritual version and those marked will be those who are his and the righteous who refuse the mark will be killed.

The Antichrist will write his name as Jesus wrote His name with the spiritual ink, the Antichrist will counter with the demonic ink via technology.

III. Solving the Riddle of Revelation 13:18- Counting the Number of His Name

The end of the riddle tells us to count the number of his name. In the term numbering of his name we see this nearly exact term in the book of numbers: These verses are as follows:

Numbers 1:2 *Take ye the sum of all the congregation of the children of Israel after families, by the house of their fathers with the number of their names, every male by their polls.*

Numbers 3:40 *And the Lord said unto Moses, Number all the firstborn of males of the children of Israel from a month old and upward and take the number of their names*

We read in Revelation:17, the elaboration on the number of his name.

Revelation 13:17 *and that no one could not buy or sell unless they had the mark, which is the name of the beast or the number of his name.*

We see counting the number of their names as simple as counting the sum of the names and adding them up. But in the mark of the Beast, the number does not apply to a group of persons but to one person: the Antichrist.

IV. Jesus Warns of Life in the Antichrist's Police State

In addressing the Ethical Assessment of Implantable Brain chips, an expert stated:

The most frightening implication of this technology is the grave possibility that it would facilitate totalitarian control of humans. In a prescient projection of experimental protocols, George Annas writes of the "project to implant removable monitoring devices at the base of the brain of neonates in three major teaching hospitals....The devices would not only permit us to locate all the implanted at any time, but could be programmed in the future to monitor the sound around them and to play subliminal messages directly to their brains." Using such technology governments could control and monitor citizens.

Another scientist stated that while seeing all of the benefits of the technology, this use for it is what kept him up at night.

Jesus gave us insight into the Antichrist's police state, he foretold in

Mark 13:12-13, *"¹²Now brother will betray brother to death, and a father his child; and children will rise up against parents and cause them to be put to death.¹³ And you will be hated by all for My name's sake. But he who endures to the end shall be saved."*

We already see in the Islamic State, fathers killing daughters, and brothers joining in and family members turning over other family members to death. A son turned in his mother for not wanting him to join the Islamic State and she was publically executed with her son overseeing the execution. Only, the Antichrist is going to expect allegiance to him and he will get it especially after setting up his cloned image that has life and he deceives the world into believing man has achieved immortality.

Jesus states that he who endures to the end will be saved, meaning that if you take the mark and connect to the Antichrist and take his name and become one with him or unite with him you will lose any chance at salvation. The only way to achieve salvation is to defy the Antichrist. Those who do will go through the fiery furnace and the ten days of tribulation when they are arrested and will wait to be beheaded in the temple. They will find themselves in the lion's den, which is the den of Satan, of the Antichrist who has the mouth of a lion, but Jesus tells them to not fear those who can harm the body but have no power over the soul.

The Antichrist in the first three and a half years of his reign will raise the EU to its pinnacle of power. While he leads the EU he will also be skilled at dealing with the world's problems. The plagues of God will begin to be unleashed and he will deal with these as a world leader.

Sometime during the first three and a half years, probably toward the end, he will receive a fatal wound and come back to life only it is now Satan himself who is indwelling the Antichrist's body and he goes from being the seventh to the eighth head of the Revelation. The False Prophet arises who might be a religious leader or a scientist. A good deal of money is used to now commission the making of the avatar of the Antichrist. When the image is completed and stands in the Holy of Holies, the Antichrist will claim to be God.

Daniel 7:25 foretells:

He shall speak pompous words against the Most High, Shall persecute the saints of the Most High, And shall intend to change times and law. Then the saints will be given into his hand For a time and times and half a time.

The times and laws that the Antichrist will change will be as follows in his police state:

All religion is to be destroyed and the only faith is to be in him.

The internet will be controlled by him and censorship of the internet will begin. All references to God, Jesus and terms for religions around the globe will be deleted.

Daniel 11:36-39 confirms him establishing himself as God.

[36] "Then the king shall do according to his own will: he shall exalt and magnify himself above every god, shall speak blasphemies against the God of gods, and shall prosper till the wrath has been accomplished; for what has been determined shall be done. [37] He shall regard neither the God of his fathers nor the desire of women, nor regard any god; for he shall exalt himself above them all.
[38] But in their place he shall honor a god of fortresses; and a god which his fathers did not know he shall honor with gold and silver, with precious stones and pleasant things.[39] Thus he shall act against the strongest fortresses with a foreign god, which he shall acknowledge, and advance its glory; and he shall cause them to rule over many, and divide the land for gain.

This strange, foreign god that his fathers did not know is the god of this technology for his police state, which connects him to his people and numbers 666. It is this thing, this computer mind, people controlling thing that looks like him that he places in the holy of holies as its home as if to say he is god.

To take the mark will mean that you will be directed and controlled by him or his government and they will know your every move, thought and they will be able to put their thoughts into your mind.

To accept this mark, you worship him and give yourself over to him and his government, i.e. is the beast. He will seek out those who do not take the mark to kill them and it will be nearly impossible to hide with the technologies that will be enacted.

They will find the non-mark takers, i.e. the Christians via the family members who turn them in, via the internet, camera surveillance, technology that can see through walls, drones that will find the non-mark takers hiding behind walls and in buildings.

This is why Jesus said to *flee to the mountains*, in Matthew 26:14 because in the rural mountains they can hide and there will not be easy internet access.

This flight will occur during an already difficult time of great violence, as Revelation 6 predicts that men will kill one another and even the animals that are not killers of men will mutilate men and women. There will be famine, and the unleashing of Gods plagues. The violence, brutality and sexual immorality will be at its height. Once the Antichrist declares that he is God and places his avatar in the holy of holies the violence skyrockets as he murders all those of religion especially Christians and Jews while also invading various countries. It is very likely he will behead Christians in the Jewish Temple. He will change times and laws. This is where Jesus said that if those days were not cut short there would be no faith left on the earth. During these years, the 144 thousand witnesses evangelize and finally the two witnesses near the time of the end who the world will hate.

V. The Antichrist Will Give You Two Choices For the Mark

The Antichrist will give you the choice to take the mark or not take it. There is currently a brain to brain technology that will not work if the patient does not allow it. It might be that the mark will not work as effectively or that he will give a choice. If there was no choice and it was mandatory for all then they would just chip those who say no to the mark and we would not see the martyrs under the alter in

Revelation Chapter 6 and also the passages of those who take the mark going to hell would not be written.

The second choice you are given if you accept the mark is the location or which mark. There might even be a recital or a pledge taken as the mark is taken as we saw in the worship of Nebuchadnezzar's dream image. Those are the two choices.

It will be all or nothing, you give Antichrist your all by this act, or you will be killed and in being killed will gain eternal life with the Lord Jesus Christ.

As we get closer to the Tribulation, parts of prophecy that we could not understand are now becoming clear. It is getting so close now that if you do not know Jesus you had better make sure you know Him and if you are a believer you haven't much time left to serve our Lord and Savior.

13
The Image of the Beast-The Siege of Jerusalem

The Antichrist will sign a peace treaty with Israel, guaranteeing the nation's peace, but at midway three and a half years later in the middle of the seven year tribulation is when Jerusalem comes under siege. Simultaneously with the Antichrist setting up his image in the Jewish Temple, or after the Antichrist's declaration, armies will surround Jerusalem. No one will anticipate this event even though many will be aware of the construction of the "image" because sometime towards the middle of the Tribulation, the Antichrist suffers his fatal wound and survives and the False Prophet commissions the building of the image, but no one expects what will occur at its completion or Jesus would not have issued so many warnings regarding this image. Believers living during the Tribulation should be able to piece together the signs and the 144 thousand witnesses will be preaching about the times as a warning along with teaching the Gospel.

When the image is launched in the Third Temple, and the Antichrist gives his speech and proclaims his deity, he will already have arranged for armies to surround Jerusalem to destroy the Jews and he takes Jerusalem as his headquarters. Daniel 11:45 predicts and affirms," *And he shall plant the tents of his palace between the seas and the glorious holy mountain, yet he shall come to his end, and no one will help him.*"

Jesus describes the suddenness of the siege, and the severity of it. The abomination of desolation, with the image of the beast placed in it, is the marker. Jesus warned in Matthew 24:16-22:

15 "Therefore when you see the 'abomination of desolation,'[d] spoken of by Daniel the prophet, standing in the holy place" (whoever reads, let him understand), 16 "then let those who are in Judea flee to the mountains. 17 Let him who is on the housetop not go down to take anything out of his house. 18 And let him who is in the field not go back to get his clothes.
19 But woe to those who are pregnant and to those who are nursing babies in those days! 20 And pray that your flight may not be in winter or on the Sabbath. 21 For then there will be great tribulation, such as has not been since the beginning of the world until this time, no, nor ever shall be. 22

Here we see the marker of the abomination of desolation, i.e. the avatar like robot presented in the temple as the timing of the siege of Jerusalem. So severe is the attack that Jesus tells the Jews living in Jerusalem to flee to the mountains, and if they are on the rooftop they are not go after any of their belongings and if they are in a field they are not to even run back and get their clothes. In Matthew the armies surrounding Jerusalem are not mentioned, just the timing of the forces, We get the detail of the army in Luke 21:20-38, which reads:

20 "But when you see Jerusalem surrounded by armies, then know that its desolation is near. 21 Then let those who are in Judea flee to the mountains, let those who are in the midst of her depart, and let not those who are in the country enter her. 22 For these are the days of vengeance, that all things which are written may be fulfilled.
23 But woe to those who are pregnant and to those who are nursing babies in those days! For there will be great distress in the land and wrath upon this people. 24 And they will fall by the edge of the sword, and be led away captive into all nations. And Jerusalem will be trampled by Gentiles until the times of the Gentiles are fulfilled.

In Luke we see Jesus also tell the Jews to flee to the mountains, and for those who are in Jerusalem to not enter the city and those in it to leave. We also see the woe to those who are pregnant or nursing because fleeing the war will be much more difficult for young mothers or mothers to be. Matthew adds an interesting verse, *"And pray that your flight may not be in the winter or on the Sabbath."* What is first to be noted is that Jesus tells them to pray that their flight not be in the winter or on the Sabbath, this tells us that these particular Jews know the prophecy and are aware they are in the Tribulation and that the abomination of desolation, siege of Jerusalem and mark of the Beast are coming. Concerning their flight in winter, Israel has mild winters of about 40 to 65 degrees, but with little belongings, the nights can be cold and uncomfortable without blankets and sufficient clothing and in the mountains where Jesus tells them to flee, it can get as cold as 34 degrees at night.

On the Sabbath Israel shuts down and many of the stores are closed, which would make it easier for an invading army to capture those fleeing, and to take over the city.

With the setting up of the avatar or image of the Beast in the Third Temple, and the Antichrist's proclamation of his deity, he will launch a surprise attack and surround the city with troops to overtake it and make it his headquarters.

Daniel 11:31 states, *And forces shall be mustered by him, and they shall defile the sanctuary fortress; then they shall take away the daily sacrifices, and place there the abomination of desolation."*

Daniel 8:12, *Because of transgression, an army was given over to the horn to oppose the daily sacrifices; and he cast truth to the ground. He did all of this and prospered.*

Zechariah 13-9-10 tells us *"That two-thirds in it shall be cut off and die, But one-third shall be left in it: I will bring the one-third thought the fire, Will refine them as silver is refined And test them as gold is tested. They will call upon my name, And I will answer them. I will say, "This is my people; And each one will say, The Lord is my God."*

The following verses speak of the broken covenant with Israel. The Antichrist who promised the nation peace has now taken it siege and set up his headquarters and expanded his empire to their land. The following verses are also biblical prophecies regarding the siege.

Isaiah 33:7-22:

⁷ Surely their valiant ones shall cry outside,
The ambassadors of peace shall weep bitterly.
⁸ The highways lie waste,
The traveling man ceases.
He has broken the covenant,
He has despised the cities,
He regards no man.
⁹ The earth mourns and languishes,
Lebanon is shamed and shriveled;
Sharon is like a wilderness,
And Bashan and Carmel shake off their fruits.

Psalm 55:20-21:

²⁰ He has put forth his hands against those who were at peace with him;
He has broken his covenant.
²¹ The words of his mouth were smoother than butter,
But war was in his heart;
His words were softer than oil,
Yet they were drawn swords.

Within these passages we also see the outcome of the attack, *"the ambassadors of peace weeping bitterly"* signifying the wailing of great loss, *"the highways lie waste"* meaning it will look like a war zone, *"the traveling man ceases"* meaning that it is in such a state no one will dare travel to it, the Antichrist is referred to as breaking the covenant by this act, as hating the cities because he destroys them and regarding no man meaning he has no regard for human life. The disaster is so great that the Earth itself is depicted as mourning and languishing and the city becomes a wilderness. Psalm 55 relays this as an act of war. In Revelation 12:15 the attack is compared to the force of a flood.

Joel 1:6 might also fit this invasion especially with the reference to the teeth of a lion, the Revelation describes the Antichrist as having the mouth of a lion. Joel 1:6 to 7 foretells:

For a nation has come up against My land, Strong and without number; His teeth are the teeth of a lion, He has laid waste my vine, And ruined my fig tree; He has stripped it bare and thrown it away; Its branches are made white.

While the Antichrist attacks Israel a good part of the world worships the Image of the Beast, while the mark of the Beast and his police state is instituted. It is possible that at the setting up of the avatar and the accompanying speech, which the Bible refers to as the mark of the Beast that his plans for that technology to be instituted are laid out and he lets the populace know what to expect. He will also launch his campaign against all religions and seek to destroy them along with the Jews.

It will be at this time that internet censorship of all that has to do with Jesus Christ, the Bible, and Christianity and all that the Antichrist feels opposes him will be censored from the internet and anyone posting anything contrary to his empire will be arrested.

I.   Run From the Mark of the Beast to The Mountains

When Jesus instructed the Jews to flee to the mountains, usually in mountain ranges and rural areas the internet access is poor to nonexistent, although via satellite and other methods being explored internet will be available worldwide. There is also the capability to live off of the land to survive. Those fleeing will have to go off of the grid, and go underground. A gentleman by the name of Mike wrote this to me and he couldn't be more on point, he stated, " From my point of view, another way to live without the mark of the beast is to simply head to the nearest tropical rainforest with some live fruits and vegetable plants, a tent, a canoe or small sailboat, and basically live as a fugitive for seven years. A fugitive literally from the Antichrist.

We see in Revelation Chapter 12 the depiction of the woman who is Israel fleeing the dragon given the wings of an eagle to fly into the wilderness and it states in verse 16 that *"But the earth helped the woman, and the earth opened up its mouth and swallowed up the great flood which the dragon had spewed out of his mouth."* This sounds like a giant sinkhole that will help these believers along and not only deal with the troops but also protect them.

This is where the book of Daniel tells us that *"the people who know their God shall be strong, and carry out great exploits, And those of the people who understand shall instruct many.* " The passage continues,

Yet for many days they shall fall by sword and flame, by captivity and plundering. Now when they fall, they shall be aided with a little help; but many shall join with them by intrigue. And some of those of understanding shall fall, to refine them, purify them, and make them white, until the time of the end; because it is still for the appointed time (Daniel 11:33-35.)

Note- beheadings in Revelation 20:4
Ten Days of Tribulation-Prison mentioned in Revelation 2:10
Jesus's warning in Revelation 2:10, "*Do not fear any of those things you are about to suffer. Indeed the devil is about to throw some of you into prison that you may be tested and you will have tribulation ten days. Be faithful until death, and I will give you the crown of life.*"

This also lines with Revelation 12:17.

The book of Revelation continues," *And the dragon was enraged with the woman, and he went to make war with the rest of her offspring, who keep the commandments of God and have the testimony of Jesus Christ.* Notice the emphasis on keeping the commandments of God in addition to having the testimony of Jesus Christ, taking the mark of the Beast is in direct violation of commandments one and two of the ten commandments because the act worships the Antichrist and his avatar.

This enduring until death or until the end of their life is also spoken of by Jesus in Matthew 24:13, *"But he who endures to the end will be saved."*

II. Mass Betrayals Against Those Who Refuse to Take The Mark of the Beast

As the believers run for the hills and go underground and achieve some success in hiding, a weapon in the Antichrist's arsenal will be the people who know them, turning them in.

Daniel 11:32 states: *Those who do wickedly against the covenant he shall corrupt with flattery; but the people who know their God shall be strong, and carry out great exploits.*

The word for flattery in the Hebrew means fine promises, which indicates that the Antichrist will offer some kind of a reward. We see in the verses below that family members betray family members to death. Daniel 11:30 states…*So he shall return and show regard for those who forsake the holy covenant."*

Mark 13:12 tells us:
Now brother will betray brother to death, and a father his child; and children will rise up against parents and cause them to be put to death.

Matthew 10:21 states:
Now brother will deliver up brother to death, and a father his child; and children will rise up against parents and cause them to be put to death.

Luke 12:53 adds:
Father will be divided against son and son against father, mother against daughter and daughter against mother, mother-in-law against her daughter-in-law and daughter-in-law against her mother-in-law.

Matthew 24:9-13 describes:

Then they will deliver you up to tribulation and kill you, and you will be hated by all nations for My name's sake. And then many will be offended, will betray one another, and will hate one another. Then many false prophets will rise up and deceive many. And because lawlessness will abound the love of many will grow cold. But he who endures to the end will be saved.

Jesus points to the sinful climate of the times with, *"And because lawlessness will abound the love of many will grow cold,"* which aligns with the brutality and lawlessness of the end times described in 2 Timothy 3:1-6, which we are already seeing.

It is not uncommon to hear in the radical Islamic world of a father killing his daughter, and brothers killing their sister and even turning against their mothers. In poor countries in South America mothers sell their daughters to sex slavery to pay off debt and here in America, mothers give their daughters over to drug dealers to be used sexually for drugs and give them over to their stepfathers for abuse. All of these are symptoms of the end times in which we live and are beginning to mirror the mass betrayals that Jesus describes, only at that time, sin will be at its height and the betrayals more numerous and shocking than today.

III. Torture and Death for those who don't take the Mark of the Beast

We see a particular theme in the book of Daniel and the Revelation. Daniel 11: 35 states:

"And some of those of understanding, (remember we see this word in Revelation for the riddle and mark of the beast) shall fall to refine them, purify them and make them white until the time of the end.

Daniel 12:10, *"Many shall be purified, made white, and refined but the wicked shall do wickedly; and none of the wicked shall understand but the wise shall understand."* (From here a time frame is given, the next verse begins, *"From the time that the daily sacrifices is taken away and the abomination is set up, there shall be one thousand two hundred and ninety days.*

It should also be noted that Jesus worded *"deliver you up to tribulation and kill you"* and it might be a reference to the ten days of tribulation of Revelation 2:10, meaning that there might be a process the person goes through before they are murdered and it might involve torture. Jesus instructs in Revelation 2:10, *"Be faithful until death, and I will give you the crown of life."*

Notice that in the Daniel verses I sited the reference to "and some of those of understanding" and *"none of the wicked shall understand but the wise shall understand"* and how this lines with the riddle of Revelation 13:18 *Here is wisdom,. Let him who has understanding calculate the number of the beast, for it is the number of a man: His number is 666.*

These have the understanding and wisdom and for this reason do not take the mark of the Beast and they pay with their lives.

The Bible tells us of the martyrs in Revelation 12:11: *And they overcame him by the blood of the Lamb and by the word of their testimony, and they did not love their lives to the death.*

We see again in Revelation 6:9-12 the martyrs each of them given a white robe. They are slain "for the word of God and the testimony which they held. They cry for vengeance for those on the earth who took their life and God tells them, *"That they should rest a little while longer, until both the number of their fellow servants and their brethren, who would be killed as they were, was completed."*

I wrote in an article that the reason that God allows the martyrdom of Christians in the Tribulation is because when God was going to destroy Sodom and Gomorrah Abraham prayed for the city and God let it be known that He would not destroy the city if there were any righteous in it and neither will He destroy the earth if one righteous person remained and the number God refers to in Revelation six is the final number of those remaining righteous persons.. The prophet Daniel asked when would the fulfillment of these things occur and Jesus, who is speaking in Daniel 12 confirmed, *"When the power of the holy people has been completely shattered, all these things shall be finished,"* and this also lines with Daniel 8:24, *He shall destroy the mighty and also the holy people.*

Daniel 7: 25 states:

He shall speak pompous words against the Most High, Shall persecute the saints of the Most High, And shall intend to change times and law. Then the saints shall be given into his hand For a time and times and half a time.

Daniel 7:21, *I was watching; and the same horn was making war against the saints and prevailing against them.* The next verse is noteworthy, *"until the Ancient of Days came and a judgement was made in favor of the saints of the Most High, and the time came for the saints to possess the kingdom* (this occurs with the destruction of the earth and the return of Christ.) We see this theme repeated further down in Daniel 7:26-27, indicating that the end of this king's reign is the end of the world.

We see the Antichrist accomplishing him aims and prospering in Daniel 8:12, which states, *"he did all this and prospered."*

With many of the verses of the death of the saints we see the time frame of a time, times and a half a time.

Revelation 13:14 states of the woman, which is Israel in the wilderness, *"But the woman was given two wings of a great eagle, that she might fly into the wilderness to her place, where she is nourished for a time and times and half a time, from the presence of the serpent.* It is this time frame that the martyrs are being killed and their murders are completed at the 1260th day, three and a half year point, second half of the final seven years of the 490 years of Jeremiah the prophet onto the nation of Israel.

IV. The 1290 Days of Daniel-30 Days of Bowl Judgements

The book of Daniel tells us that from the abomination of desolation is 1290 days. In the additional 30 days the angels unleash the seven bowl judgements from the seven trumpets. There is the possibility that the first bowl will overlap and be unleashed while the remaining believers are being murdered. The first bowl falls on those who have taken the mark of the beast and they receive pains and loathsome sores and from this time we see the rest of the bowl judgments of God, which might be unleashed simultaneously:
The bowl judgements in Revelation 16: 1-21 are as follows:

1. Sores on those with mark of the Beast
2. The sea becomes actual blood and all living creatures die
3. All rivers and springs become actual blood-these plagues are retribution for the martyrs, The Bible explains in the passage, *"For they have shed the blood of saints and prophets, And you have given them blood to drink. For it is their just due.*
4. The sun scorches men with great heat and fire
5. Darkness on the throne of the Beast
6. Spirits drawing and gathering armies for the battle of

Armageddon
7. A great earthquake divides cities around the globe, mountains disappear from the resulting landslides, and islands fall into the sea. Meanwhile the Earth gets pounded with 100 pound hailstones,

In support of the 30 day time frame of the bowl judgements, William F. Dankenbring commentated in an article that God's period of "judgment" will last *"one hour."* He further stated, " These ten kings give their power to the Beast for precisely "ONE HOUR." How long is "one hour," speaking prophetically?" He added.

Jesus Christ said that there are "twelve hours in a day" (John 11:9). Since a "day" equals a "year" in being fulfilled (Num.14:34; Ezek.4:4-6), and since there are 12 months in a year, Dankenbring concluded, "this means that "ONE HOUR" equals *ONE MONTH* in being fulfilled! *One month equals 30 days!"* Within this time frame we also see the destruction of Babylon in Revelation 17.

I don't know if anyone will be able to imagine how horrible this final 30 days will be, it begins with suffering from the loathsome and very painful sores on all of those marked with the mark of the Beast. As the last Christian is murdered, all oceans, seas, rivers, lakes, streams and dams will turn to actual blood and the life within those bodies of water will die and pile on beaches. This is God's retaliation for the killing of his saints for their not taking the mark of the beast.

Once the waters are turned to blood and all sea life dies so will all other animal life, causing famine and thirst on top of the sores. The entire ecosystem will be out of whack causing all kinds of horrors.

If this is not bad enough, right after the waters turn to blood, the sun will become extremely hot, so hot that it will cause fires and men will be burned by the heat of the sun possibly resulting from the sun's nuclear fusion creating more helium and there will be no water to quench their thirst. The great heat will cause massive power outages as circuits go on overload, and men and women will be thirsty, hot and dealing with their sores.

There will be rioting and fighting as people fight and loot for something to drink. There will be mass panic. The extreme sun will add more horrors to already disrupted eco system.

The Antichrist's kingdom turns to darkness and the River Euphrates dries up. Three frog like spirits each one out of the unholy trinity's mouth will go out to assemble the armies of the world to the valley of Megiddo, i.e. that is Armageddon. It should be noted that frogs group, and groups of frogs are called armies. In the Revelation we see three separate frogs coming out of the mouth of each member of the unholy trinity, getting the armies of the world to group just as frogs group in armies. Satan knows that Christ will be coming in the clouds and his aim is to defeat Christ by this massive army.

It should be noted that there will not be the population numbers on the earth that started at the beginning of the Tribulation, as a result of the Revelation plagues and the Antichrist's conquests. Some writers have tried to estimate the numbers based on the estimates of the numbers of dead given in the books of the prophets, but the number will nowhere be near the over 7.4 billion that exists now.

V. Possible Reasons for the battle of Armageddon

Jeremiah 6:22-23 states, *"Behold a people comes from the north country, And a great nation will be raised from the farthest parts of the earth. They will lay hold on bow and spear; They are cruel and have no mercy; Their voice roars like the sea; And they ride on horses, As men of war set in array against you, O daughter of Zion."* This could be Russia and the United States going to the battle of Armageddon, as the US fits the description of a great nation from the farthest parts of the Earth in relation to Israel. The Antichrist will be engaged in various battles that Daniel 11 predict with the king of the North and South that is one of the African nations. It is not Egypt, Libya, or Ethiopia because these nations are mentioned as nations falling to the Antichrist and his occupation. It could possibly be South Africa that stands up against the Antichrist invading the continent and taking over various nations. The invading armies can be going against the Antichrist because of the sores from his mark and he loses his luster in the eyes of the world. It could also be because of his invasion of the nations, which is recorded in Isaiah 10:13-14:

By the strength of my hand I have done it, And by my wisdom, for I am prudent; Also I have removed the boundaries of the people, And have robbed their treasuries; So I have put down the inhabitants like a valiant man. My hand has found like a nest the riches of the people, And as one gathers eggs that are left, I have gathered all the earth; And there was no one who moved his wing, Nor opened his mouth with even a peep.

Upon the completion of the seventh bowl, which is the great earthquake that divides cities around the globe and causes worldwide landslides, tsunamis and 100 pound hail, the armies of the world surround Jerusalem.

VI. The Cataclysmic End of the World and Return of Christ

Jesus said in Matthew 24:29-31, and *"immediately after the tribulation of those days, "the sun will be darkened, and the moon will not give its light; the stars will fall from heaven, and the powers of the heavens will be shaken. Then the sign of the Son of Man will appear in heaven, and then all of the tribes will mourn, they will see the Son of man coming in the clouds of heaven with power and great glory. And He will send His angels with a great sound of a trumpet, and they will gather together His elect from the four winds, from one end of heaven to the other."*

Immediately after the pouring onto the Earth of the bowl judgments, the sun and moon will be darkened. The darkening can occur from the sun's previous state of getting so hot that it burned up all of its energy, and with the darkening of the sun comes the blood moon to finally the moon dimming and the stars will fall from heaven possibly from the sun going out. The Earth without the sun will get bitter cold below freezing. The Earth will go off its orbit and the falling stars will obliterate the Earth (Isaiah 24:19-20). Jesus appears in the clouds with the saints and the trumpet sounds with the gathering of the elect and the current physical world as we know it ceases to exist.

14

The Technology god In The Book of Daniel

This report establishes that the technology god of the end times is predicted in Daniel 11:38-39, which reads:

*³⁸ But in their place he shall honor a **god of fortresses**; and a god which his fathers did not know he shall honor with gold and silver, with precious stones and pleasant things. ³⁹ Thus he shall act against the strongest fortresses with a foreign god, which he shall acknowledge, and advance its glory; and he shall cause them to rule over many, and divide the land for gain.*

I have already elaborated established regarding this verse how technology is a newer god, which is why in this passage it is referred to as *"a god which his fathers did not know."* The Antichrist will *"advance its glory,"* because this god advances him and allows him to enact his police state and so much more. This is why the verse reads, *"and he shall cause them to rule over many."* The word used for rule in the original language means cause to rule, to give dominion.

The word for fortresses, or forces used in verse 38--within the phrase god of fortresses-- is not the usual word used for forces, which means: strength, power, might or armies, ability or efficiency. We automatically would think of an army or a fortress, but rather the word used for forces is a word used meaning: a place of safety, protection, stronghold, and it is a word used for God Himself as our refuge and strength. Psalm 31:2 states, *"Be though my strong rock,"* with strong being the same word that is used in Daniel 11:38-39. Psalm 28:8 reads, *"The LORD is their strength and he is the saving strength of his anointed."* With strength of his anointed using the same word as is used in Daniel 11:38-39. Thus the god of fortresses offers God like protection, or a God like quality, which can be said of the technology used for a police state.

I. The Technology god And Its Prophets

The technology god that has emerged, exists within a set of doctrines and beliefs. Although many scientists are atheists their beliefs sound more far-fetched than the biblical teachings that they refute. While some of their science is based on fact, a good deal is based on theories. Along with science comes science fiction and some scientists are entrenched in both. It is notable that many can tell you scenes out of the latest Sci-Fi movies, and out of Star Trek, but they have no knowledge of the Bible.

The technology god prophets called futurists advocate technology as the end all and have gone so far as to talk about technology ending humanity and creating a new immortal race, or artificial intelligence taking over humanity.

No one captured the idea of technology as god more precisely than quantum computing D-Wave founder Eric Ladizinsky, when he spoke of the pulse like noise of the D-Wave machine sounding like a heartbeat and called it "an alter to an alien god."

The chief prophet is author, inventor, futurist, computer scientist Ray Kurzweil, who in 1988 was named the Inventor of the Year by MIT, was awarded the Dickson Prize, Carnegie Melon's top science prize in 1994, in 1999 won the United States' highest honor in technology the National Medal of Technology and Innovation in 2001 the Lemelson-MIT Prize, and in 2002 inducted into the U.S. Patent Office's National Inventor's Hall of Fame. In addition, Kurzweil was the recipient of nine honorary doctorates.

Ray Kurzweil is the science world's leading prophet on the merging of man with machines as the creation of a new race. Kurzweil is an advocate for the futurist and transhumanist movements, which include the future of nanotechnology, robotics and biotechnology. He is a leading teacher on the technological singularity.

Kurzweil's books include: *The Age of Spiritual Machines, The Singularity is Near,* and *How to Create a Mind the Secret of Human Thought Revealed.*

He stated of the singularity, "Technological change will be so rapid and its impact so profound that every aspect of human life will be irreversibly transformed…There won't be a clear distinction between humans and machines…Computers are not going to be these rectangular devices…They are going to be inside our body and brain and we are going to be a hybrid of biological and non-biological intelligence. Go back 500 years, not a lot happened. Now a lot happens in six months. Technology feeds on itself and it gets faster and faster. The future changes will be so rapid you won't be able to follow it unless you merge with it."

Based on Ray Kurzweil's book, *The Age of Spiritual Machines: When Computers Exceed Human Intelligence,* and his talks, he believes that these machines possess human consciousness and a soul. He stated, "By 2020, we will begin to have relationships with automated personalities and use them as teachers, companions, and lovers. By 2030, the distinction between us and computers will have been so sufficiently blurred that when machines claim to be conscious, we will have no choice but to believe them. Human identity will be called into question as never before, as a billion years of evolution are superseded in a mere hundred by machine technology that we have created. We will become cyborgs, but what will computers become?"

There is also this idea that the machines will adopt the best traits of humans as they develop. Another prophet of the technology god, Ben Goertzel, PhD., is an American author and researcher in the field of artificial intelligence. His positions include chief scientist, scientific adviser and chairman for robotics and biopharma companies and artificial intelligence and futurist societies, along with being an adviser to Singularity University and is also research professor in the Fujian Key Lab for Brain-Like Intelligent Systems at Xiamen University, China.

Goertzel stated in line with this idea, "People have this idea that computers robots somehow have to be cold and impersonal and uncaring, I don't see why that's true, I believe we can go to artificial machines that are more caring, more compassionate, have better and stable goal systems than a human being. Once machines can think better than us all these other technologies will develop faster and faster."

Futurist Max Moore, PhD., who founded the Extrophy Institute, wrote on becoming post human, "were saying that we can become something more than human… challenging every orthodox belief, challenging what we currently accept and saying why can't we do better? Why can't we improve human biology? Why can't we change our genome? Just because it is the way it is doesn't mean it's as good as it can be. Why do we age and die why can't we do something about that?

Futurist, theoretical physicist and also technology god prophet Michio Kaku stated that at MIT they are trying to create emotional robots. The idea is that technology can enhance humans, create an entire new race and achieve immortality.

Although the god of technology has its own teachings on artificial intelligence and a post human race, these will feed into the Antichrist's claims. He will not adopt these teachings but will adapt them to his claims of deity and to blaspheme God. Daniel 7:25 tells us he will change times and laws and will sanction what has been deemed unethical. The False Prophet will be his greatest advocate and as I stated before, may very well be a scientist.

II. The Technology gods Teachings, Buzzwords and Mark of the Beast

As with any teachings, there are doctrines and buzzwords. Some of these have filled the airwaves of Bible prophecy talk shows in discussions of the mark of the Beast. They are as follows.

Transhumanism is an international and intellectual movement that aims to transform the human condition by developing and making widely available sophisticated technologies to greatly enhance human intellectual, physical, and psychological capacities. The Nano biotechnological enhancement of human beings.

The Singularity (technological singularity) is the hypothesis that the invention of artificial superintelligence will abruptly trigger runaway technological growth, resulting in unfathomable changes to human civilization

Cyborgs (short for "**cyb**ernetic **org**anism") is a being with both organic and bio mechatronic body parts.

Dr. Oskar Aszmann removed a young man's paralyzed non-working hand, destroyed after a tragic accident, and replaced it with a fully operational machine computerized version. Dr. Oskar Aszmann commented at the end of his "Ted Talk" titled, "What if we become trans humans?" that he had created a cyborg.

Post Humans is a concept originating in the fields of science fiction, futurology, contemporary art, and philosophy that literally means a person or entity that exists in a state beyond being human.

Extropianism, also referred to as the philosophy of *Extropy*, is an evolving framework of values and standards for continuously improving the human condition.

Chimeras, a **genetic chimerism** or **chimera** is a single organism composed of cells from different zygotes. In Greek mythology, a Chimera was a monstrous fire-breathing hybrid creature composed of the parts of more than one animal.

Nanotechnology ("**nanotech**") is manipulation of matter on an atomic, molecular, and supramolecular scale.

Biotechnology is the use of living systems and organisms to develop or make products or any technological application that uses biological systems, living organisms or derivatives thereof, to make or modify products or processes for specific use.

Avatar-- in computing--an avatar is the graphical representation of the user or the user's alter ego or character. It may take a three-dimensional form.

While this list is not exhaustive, it includes the main topics and categories spoken of by the technology god prophets.

III. Miracles Duplicated By Technology god

In end time Bible Prophecy we see the prediction of a good deal of miracles. Jesus predicted in Matthew 24:24, *24 For false christ's and false prophets will rise and show great signs and wonders to deceive, if possible, even the elect.*
We also see miracles performed by the False Prophet and in this environment God sends the two olive branches, which are Moses and Elijah or some believe could be Elijah and Enoch, and they perform miracles.

We see an interesting aspect of the technology god and that is the ability of technology to seemingly perform miracles. Nanotechnology, which can produce object from atoms appears to produce miracles, and is predicted to create any object you could want to create from food to furniture, to rebuilding damaged organs in the body.

Bill Joy, co-founder of Sun Microsystems stated that carbon nanotubes, which were created in 1991, are the "strongest material known... 30 times stronger than Kevlar, they repair themselves in phantom seconds, if you shine a light they produce electricity, if you shine a light on them they emit fire." He added that you can run a 1000 times more current through them than a piece of metal and they have several other amazing properties.

Holograms can make someone appear in a room who is miles away, and also duplicate fire coming down from heaven.

Ray Kurtzweil, stated that in the near future we will be able to send a hug and a kiss from miles away.

Who knows what will be next, but these technological feats might be inclusive in those that could possibly deceive the very elect.

15
Technology Tower of Babel

A noteworthy characteristic of the end time technology god is that it springs from a Tower of Babel mindset or endeavor. As the age nears to drawing to a close we are seeing once again the building of a Tower of Babel the in the area of technology.

The Tower of Babel account in Genesis 11:1-9 begins by stating, *"Now the whole earth had one language and one speech."*

It continues:

[4] And they said, "Come, let us build ourselves a city, and a tower whose top is in the heavens; let us make a name for ourselves, lest we be scattered abroad over the face of the whole earth."
[5] But the LORD came down to see the city and the tower which the sons of men had built. [6] And the LORD said, "Indeed the people are one and they all have one language, and this is what they begin to do; now nothing that they propose to do will be withheld from them.[7]
Come, let Us go down and there confuse their language, that they may not understand one another's speech." [8] So the LORD scattered them abroad from there over the face of all the earth, and they ceased building the city. [9] Therefore its name is called Babel, because there the LORD confused the language of all the

earth; and from there the LORD scattered them abroad over the face of all the earth.

The intention of the builders of the city was to make a tower so tall that the top of the tower would reach heaven and the abode of God. They would then make a name for themselves.

The Bible states in verse 5, *"Indeed the people are one and they all have one language, and this is that they begin to do; now nothing that they propose to do will be withheld unto them."*

When the people were united, one of their first attempts was to be on par with God, and God knew that they would not accomplish this feat by building this tower because they could only build so far up into the sky. But it was the idea that being on par with God was their intention. They were looking to become great and for notoriety for themselves. How much better than to mimic God Himself.

God confused their language and scattered them and by doing so we had the division of nations identified by their languages and culture. Empires might take over some of those nations and absorb their language and culture, but overall there remained division of peoples.

At the time of Babel the Bible tells us:

"Now the whole earth had one language and one speech."

The industrial age began in 1760, followed by the machine age of 1880, which was trailed by the information age, which soured by 1990 onward. And this has brought us to the time of the end described in Daniel 12:4, which states, *"But you, Daniel, shut up the words and seal the book, until the time of the end. Many shall run to and fro, and knowledge shall increase."*

Along with increased knowledge and high speed travel, an interesting development occurred, the barriers that God created- we see in retrospect -were only temporary because we have again arrived at a time when the people are close to being one as at the time of Babel.

As industry and technology caused the world economies' to become interdependent, world problems became global in nature. This caused world leaders to unite to solve them and form global institutions to deal with the tasks.

Thus a byproduct of the machine and technological age were world institutions, interconnected economies and even the language barrier came down with translation of languages occurring at the push of a button for anything you might read on the internet. As industry and technology accelerated so did the means to teach and translate languages. Technology allowed languages to be taught easily so that one person can learn several.

The languages and nations that God established to prevent a Tower of Babel in these end times have been eradicated via technology and the nation state has eroded through globalization.

In this globalized world the EU formed along with many regional groupings, dividing our giant world like a pie and helping it unify so that groups like the one that appeared at Babel would emerge to make a name for themselves.

From these sprang the international scientific projects such as the human genome project or the brain initiatives in an effort to research and eradicate disease.

These scientists are determined to crack the code of life and learn how the brain works to mimic it in the most ungodly of ways such as uploading one's memories to a computer. Futurist Jason Sosa stated, we will "be able to delete memories and upload new ones." Scientists are also aiming to perfect on God's creation with superhuman skin, hearing and vision.

It goes beyond just helping to improve lives but has ventured into other fields and is now a Tower of Babel as man attempts to improve on God's creation and even create a new living race. There are even experiments to create motherless babies. It does not stop here as man is also as was in the actual time of Babel attempting to reach into the heavens.

I. Two Towers of Babel That Reach to the Heavens- CERN and FAST

There are other towers being built that literally like Babel are being built to connect to the heavens,

CERN has got some evangelical writers abuzz who are teaching that CERN is going into the abyss and letting out all kinds of demons and that there has even been changes to the Bible, which is not possible.

CERN is a European research organization that operates the largest particle physics laboratory in the world. CERN is also the birthplace of the World Wide Web.

The acronym CERN are the French words for European Council for Nuclear Research. It was established by 12 European governments in 1952. Several important achievements in particle physics have been made through experiments at CERN.

CERN operates a network of six accelerators and a decelerator. Each machine in the chain increases the energy of particle beams before delivering them to experiments or to the next more powerful accelerator. CERN particularly gained notoriety with the Large Hadron Collider, which represents a large-scale, worldwide scientific cooperation project.

The LHC tunnel is located 100 meters underground, in the region between the Geneva International Airport and the nearby Jura Mountains.

From their own website it states that their "physicists and engineers are probing the fundamental structure of the universe. They use the world's largest and most complex scientific instruments to study the basic constituents of matter – the fundamental particles. The particles are made to collide together at close to the speed of light. The process gives the physicists clues about how the particles interact, and provides insights into the fundamental laws of nature."

It should be noted that their work is based on theories and especially the big-bang theory. With their discovery in 2012 of the Higgs boson particle one of the two fundamental particles, proving how particles gain mass. They believe a Higg's field is all around us and that bosons carry particles. One journalist commented that the discovery disproves God, but the journalist was uninformed because the particle does not disprove God.

Evangelicals believe that the black holes, which are also not proven sound like the abyss spoken of in the Bible and that at CERN they have accessed the key to the abyss. First and foremost we do not know if this is the abyss, or the bottomless pit and only the angel with the key mentioned in the Revelation has the key. Can there be a crossover into that world? More on that in the next and chapter "Parallel Worlds."

China's Radio Telescope is another Tower of Babel venture. The Chinese Academy of Sciences Five-hundred-meter Aperture Spherical Telescope (FAST) scans the skies. First proposed in 1994, the project was green-lighted by the Chinese government in 2007, construction began in 2011 and was completed in July of 2016. With a dish 500 m across, comprising of 4450 reflecting panels, it is the largest filled in, single-dish radio telescope in the world. Its area is equal to 30 soccer fields. A Nimitz-class aircraft carrier could easily float in the 500 meter dish from bow to stern, with room to spare.

FAST probes the universe at radio wavelengths, hunting for faint pulsars, mapping neutral hydrogen in distant galaxies, and searching for signs of extraterrestrial communications and intelligence.

Shortly after it began functioning, FAST made its first observation of a pulsar 1,351 light-years away this past month. FAST like the ancient Tower of Babel builders aspired has literally build a tower that can reach toward the heavens. Will they find anything? Only the demonic activity that their machine might invite especially as we get closer to the end.

II. The Antichrist Will Head Technology Tower of Babel

It is worth noting that in these end times with the barriers that God put in place having eroded, and we see this in these various scientific endeavors, which are global, the world is more of a single unit. Once again as it was in Babel and as God stated, *"now nothing that they propose to do will be withheld unto them."*

And we see this clearly in the area of technology, where man is attempting to perfect creation and humans and recreate the human race into another species and recreate creation and reach into the heavens.

While the divisions originally set up at Babel have greatly eroded they have not completely gone and will not be completely removed until the Tribulation when the world is headed under the empire of the Antichrist. Never the less, we see the Tower of Babel mentality preparing for the Antichrist and the final completed Tower of Babel that will be spearheaded by him. From this tower the technology god assists him and life under his regime.

It should come as no surprise that we see the Tower of Babel mentality in the end times, along with the emergence of the tower and the god of technology that spearheads it, which will then utilized by the son of Satan himself. It should also be noted that it is the Dragon or Satan, who prepares for the reign of his son and has influenced the building of the technology tower and its false god and teachings.

III. Funding For Babel's Mark of the Beast in Place

The people of the Tower of Babel's ultimate goal was for notoriety and to make a name for themselves. In our modern technological Tower of Babel we see the world's empires and nations aiming for the wealth and power technological products will provide.

David Simpson, author of the *Post Human Book Series* stated it perfectly at his TED talk when he said, "Intelligence is pretty powerful, the country that attains strong AI first has dominant strategic advantage forever."

The US, China, EU and Japan are the top four spenders on research and development of new technologies. In the account of Babel, bricks were used to build the tower and in today's environment, it is money that provides for the building.

It is in this environment that the mark of the Beast will be discovered and launched. Bible prophecy allows us to know the future, and in knowing the future we can see how these actions are leading to what will be the final outcome as portrayed in the Bible.

Based on Bible prophecy we know that the future European Union will win this technological race. Since the EU is the launching pad for the Antichrist, I am going to focus on the EU's current spending.

The EU's Future and Emerging Technologies program allocates considerable funding with the mission of turning science into products and it takes the lead in yet uncharted technological territories.

The EU Commission's website it states:

"FET actions are expected to initiate radically new lines of technology through unexplored collaborations between advanced multidisciplinary science and cutting-edge engineering. It will help Europe grasp leadership early on in those promising future technology areas able to renew the basis for future European competitiveness and growth, and that can make a difference for society in the decades to come."

FET Open funds projects on new ideas for radically new future technologies, at an early stage when there are few researchers working on a project topic. FET also nurtures, supports, and helps build exploratory research topics.

The description of the types of projects that FET funds describe the image and mark of the Beast type of technologies. The EU is pouring considerable moneys into these projects to insure their success.

FET Flagships are 1-billion, 10-years initiatives, which bring together hundreds of excellent European researchers to unite forces and focus on solving ambitious scientific and technological challenges, such as the Human Brain Project, which started in 2013 and the initiative in Quantum Technology, which will begin in 2018.

The reason for the huge amount of funding into quantum technologies is in their own words to "ensure Europe's leading role in a technological revolution now under way."

The EU Commission will launch its €1 billion flagship-scale initiative in quantum technology, within the H2020 research and innovation framework programme discussed earlier in this report.

The "initiative aims to place Europe at the forefront of the second quantum revolution now unfolding worldwide, bringing transformative advances to science, industry and society and thus securing the EU's position in the world. The spending and infrastructure for the research and development of new technologies is all in place as is the quest to be the empire that makes the discovery and is the first to distribute the product. It will accomplish more than all of this, the technology will provide the Antichrist with his mark for all of society.

16
Parallel Dimensions

In science there is a good deal of emphasis and talk of parallel dimensions and of the possibility of life on other planets. In quantum computing there is the theory that quantum computers work by crossing into other dimensions.

When it comes to parallel dimensions the Bible is very clear of the parallel universe that exists alongside of ours and describes it in considerable detail.

It is almost paradoxical that that scientists have little to no knowledge of the parallel dimension described in some detail in the Bible but can tell you the details of Star Trek episodes as if it were the Bible on parallel dimensions. This world will sync with the Antichrist's mark of the Beast.

Before I discuss how the parallel dimensions relate to the mark of the Beast, one must have knowledge of the parallel dimension relayed in Scripture. The parallel universe that exists alongside ours, is depicted the most in Bible prophecy or more specifically the end time prophetic passages.

I. Parallel Universe-The God of the Bible

To comprehend it, one must first examine the God of the Bible. As an analyst and a journalist I often step back and view God as He is presented in the Bible and not as He has been stereotyped. As I study Scripture, I am often struck by the esoteric and peculiar nature of the God presented in the Bible. Too often our image of God is who we think He should be and how we think He should act. The reality is that the unusual God presented in the Bible is incomprehensible and not fully understood by our finite minds. It makes logical sense that we as humans are only possible of having limited comprehension of Him.

Many times we read the Bible and accept its words without thinking twice about the voice of God that speaks through them and what they tell us about His person. The Scriptures tell us that His ways are not our ways or His thoughts our thoughts and this is evident as we examine God as He is presented in Scripture.

First and foremost God chooses to speak to us through the Bible, which is His word. The God of the universe who created the galaxies and all life on this earth chose to leave a book and not just any writings, but His word, written through various writers, which would possess attributes of no other books or writings.

It was written over 1500 years, by 40 different authors and yet the language and theme are consistent from Genesis to Revelation. We see in the book, an esoteric God whose ways defy human reasoning. The language of the book is not only primitive, but possessing peculiar lingo, not uttered anywhere else at any time in history.

The Bible itself is a supernatural book. In addition, the words in the book have properties that no other books possess in that they are dimensional.

The parallel universe described in its pages has the feel of a Sci Fi thriller, an episode of the Twilight Zone, Star Trek, a video game theme, an action adventure, all in one. It takes you nowhere your mind has gone, or will possibly ever go. Another words you can't think up or imagine what is in the parallel dimension the Bible describes because it defies our limited logic. It does not exist in a faraway galaxy, but rather alongside our physical Earth in the air. It is also way beyond our science because science is not even close to discovering it.

It begins with God Himself. In the books of the prophets we see Him depicted in His throne room and we know that He has the image of a man and possesses emotions. Yet He is also described as a force of nature. In the new heaven and the new earth that He will create, we see that God provides the light, so there is no need of the sun. His voice is like thunder and of the sound of roaring waves.

Before God's throne are seven spirits, and four living creatures, one looking like a lion, the other a calf, the other a man and the final one an eagle with feet that look like calves feet. These do not have the ability to turn but only to walk in a forward or backward direction and they move at the speed of light, like flashes of lightening. Each has six wings with two wings stretching upward, two wings touching each other and the other two wings covering their bodies. They each have eyes covering them. Beside each creature are large wheels with rims that are covered with eyes. Everywhere the creatures go the wheels follow them. The spirit of the creatures is in these large wheels. As their wings move they make the sound of an army, and the roar of an ocean.

These winged beings praise God saying, *"Holy, holy, holy, Lord God Almighty, who was and is and is to come!"* They reside above and below the throne. The throne itself shines with the brilliance of a rainbow and He who sits on it while appearing as a man, also appears like the sun with its amber color and fire. His throne is described within a temple and the train of his robe fills the temple. Within the temple is a golden altar, with tongs, and coal and fire.

In the Revelation we learn that around the throne are 24 elders. We see Him who sits on the throne holding a scroll sealed with seven seals. We also see Jesus, depicted in linen and a golden girdle, and

His head and hair glisten white. God's temple is filled with smoke from His glory and power. As He speaks we hear noises and thunder, and we see flashes of lightening. When the scroll is opened and only the Lamb of God is worthy to open it, we see Him open the seven seals and seven judgments are released onto the Earth, but the seventh seal releases the seven angels with the seven trumpet judgements and the seventh angel releases the seven bowl judgements.

II. Parallel Universe -Demons and Angels in the Revelation

In this parallel world is described a mighty angel clothed with a cloud and a rainbow on his head, whose face is like the sun and feet like pillars of fire. He cries out as a lion cries out and when he uttered his voice seven thunders uttered their voices. He holds in his hand a little book, which the apostle John is to take from the angel and eat it, it tastes sweet but is bitter in his stomach.

In the Revelation we see even more of these figures:

The four angels bound at the River Euphrates and prepared and released to kill a third of mankind.

The beast who ascends out of the bottomless pit.

Michael, the prince over Israel whose heavenly army fights Satan and his demons in a war, which takes place in heaven.

The demonic principality named Death

The demonic principality named Hades

The angel with a key to the bottomless pit with smoke arising and darkening the sun and moon.

Locusts that sting like a scorpions emerge and they have a king whose name is Apollyon in Greek, (meaning Destroyer) Abaddon in

Hebrew. (A destroying angel)

The angel flying with the everlasting Gospel

The Angel with power over fire

Angels dressed in linen and gold girdles coming out of the temple and one of the four living creatures gives to the angels the seven bowls full of the wrath of God. After this the Revelation tells us,
"The temple was filled with the smoke from the glory of God and from His power, and no one was able to enter the temple till the seven plagues of the seven angels was completed."

Harpists playing harps

The sealed and marked 144 thousand witnesses

There is so much more in the Revelation from the new heaven and new Earth and its description: the book of life, the tree of life, the lake of fire, and the seal of Jesus Christ on the book of Revelation along with His warning. We see in the Revelation demons that are principalities and powerful angels as in no other book of the Bible. All this as God's judgements are issued from His temple in the heavens, and thus providing the greatest glimpse into the parallel world that is depicted throughout all of Scripture.

We see another view of this parallel universe in the fiery chariot with fiery horses that came for Elijah in 2 Kings 2:11, and in 2 Kings 6:8-23. In these passages God protected Elisha and his servant with angels leading horses and chariots of fire. God opened Elisha's eyes so that he could see them when ancient Aram was at war with Israel. The king sent a large group of soldiers to capture Elisha because he was able to predict to the king of Israel the armies next attack allowing the King of Israel to prepare an effective strategy.

While this is not an exhaustive study on demons and angels enough details are provided so that you can begin to get a picture of this world.

III. Parallel Universe- Understood by a Child

It all began in the garden and the fall of man. Not only did this launch the battle that will end at Armageddon, but it also reveals to us a peculiar God, who required the sacrificial blood of animals that would foreshadow the death of His Son and the blood atonement required for salvation.

This God who would send His Son into the world not as a king but as a lowly servant, who would die a most brutal death so that He would share in our sufferings and also give us life through His name. This life is eternal life and it comes by faith in His son, Jesus Christ. This God who would speak through prophets and ask them to perform seemingly peculiar acts to drive home His message.

Such as having Ezekiel cut his hair and beard, weigh it and divide it three ways. One third he was to burn with fire, one third strike with the sword and one third scatter to the wind and keep some of it out and sew into the edge of his garment, to represent and coincide with God's judgements. There are several of these throughout the book of Ezekiel. This strange God who would address Ezekiel as son of man as if talking to a species that was unlike His own, but that He created. This peculiar God who would when speaking to Ezekiel refer to Himself as the Lord of Hosts.

I think of the nazarite vow of Samson and John the Baptist. They were not to cut their hair and were not to eat any grapes or have any food products made from grapes.

The Abrahamic Covenant, the Mosaic Law, God requiring the building of a temple and providing every instruction for its construction. The blood sacrifice that would be performed and would represent and foreshadow Jesus Christ, who was coming and going to be the atonement for man's sins. Jesus who would be born of a virgin and would die a most brutal death, with every drop of His blood poured out to pay for my sins and yours and who would resurrect from death and promise all who believe in Him eternal life.

The blood sacrifice is what is incomprehensible to our rational mind and defies our human reasoning. This is required from the God of the universe? Yes, and this God requires faith to please Him and He knows that faith is difficult for man. The paradox is that it is the faith of a child that is required to understand His complexity. This is backed up in Scripture in the following verses:

Luke 18:17, *"Verily I say unto you, Whosoever shall not receive the kingdom of God as a little child shall in no wise enter therein."*

Matthew 18:3. *"And said, Verily I say unto you, Except ye be converted, and become as little children, ye shall not enter into the kingdom of heaven."*

It is not of works that we achieve eternal life and life with Christ, but through faith and belief in this fantastic foolish sounding Gospel, which is the power of a God that we cannot for the life of us comprehend. It takes childlike faith to understand it. It's like getting through a corn maze. Corn mazes are popular attractions at farms in the United States. Farmers will build mazes through their corn fields in an effort to help their farms earn money. Many people have gotten lost in the maze and some have phoned the police to help find them. One of the recommendations for finding your way out of a corn maze if you find yourself lost is to follow the kids because they somehow know how to get out of one. This is a prime example of a child having an ability that an adult does not possess such as understanding the God of the Bible.

Jesus Himself told us we would need the faith of a child to believe in Him. A child can comprehend this fantastic world and the Gospel of the Lord Jesus Christ because they do not have adult reasoning. God and His parallel world as described in the Bible defies our reasoning. Yet, because it is incomprehensible to us does not mean that it does not exist.

IV. The Parallel Dimension Connects with the Physical World

As far apart and unparalleled as the spiritual and physical world seem, they connect and exist alongside one another. This world plays out in the heavens and here on Earth and within our beings. We have a soul within our physical body. Upon our physical death our soul departs our body. The Bible tells us that the life is in the blood and somehow the soul mingles in our blood and charges every cell of our body as it would a battery.

For those us who are born again, Jesus breathed on us the Holy Spirit, which opens our eyes and we can testify as witnesses of our experiences in this spiritual world.

Satan is referred to in the Bible as the prince of the air and demons are everywhere trying to influence us. They can indwell and oppress human beings.

No two topics can seem farther apart than Bible prophecy and current events and yet in the physical world we see the fulfillment of what Bible prophecy predicts will occur in the end times.

End time Bible prophecy centers on the nation of Israel, and in 1948 Israel became a nation and only three years later was the formation of the EU, which would fulfill the prophet Daniel's predictions of a revived Roman Empire that will under the rule of the Antichrist persecute that nation.

Jesus spoke of the abomination of desolation that takes place inside of the Third Temple, and today as I write this the plans are all in place as are the utensils, clothing and all else for the building of the Third Temple. This report has provided you with how the technological advances are lining with Bible prophecy, which shows us an example of the linked spiritual and physical world.

V. Antichrist Via Technology Will Mimic the Holy Trinity

In this parallel world, the battle of the ages rages and merges under the Antichrist. These worlds will unite as Satan will use technology to mimic the Trinity and to give him his reign in the physical world.

The Antichrist will declare that he is God. The mark of the Beast will allow him to know whatever he needs to know about you and act on the information in his police state. Technology will render him omnipresent and all-knowing in the physical world.

He will replicate God's sealing of his servants and write his name on his subject's foreheads with the mark, just as God marked His servants in Revelation 22:4, which affirms, *"They shall see His face, and His name shall be on their foreheads."*

He will mimic the Holy Spirit by putting his thoughts into you and guiding you. His mark will enter into a person as the Holy Spirit does. It will teach them, direct them, counsel, guide and also know them, in the same way the Holy Spirit works in the life of the believer. This is taught in the following verses:

2 Corinthians 1:22, *"Who hath also sealed us, and given the earnest of the Spirit in our hearts."*

Ephesians 1:13, *"In whom ye also trusted, after that ye heard the word of truth, the gospel of your salvation: in whom also after that ye believed, ye were sealed with that holy Spirit of promise."*

Notice the Holy Spirit enters *"after that ye believed."* It will be the same with the mark of the Beast, you will need to believe in the Antichrist and give yourself over to him.

Ephesians 4:30 tells us, *"And do not grieve the Holy Spirit of God, by whom you were sealed for the day of redemption."* Sadly, those who take the mark will number themselves for hell's fires.

The Antichrist will mimic the Lord Jesus Christ via the mark. He will be able to go inside of the recipient and become one with them. The Antichrist will also make his subject one in him as Jesus described of Himself and His followers in John 17: 20-24:

[20] *"I do not pray for these alone, but also for those who will believe in Me through their word;* [21] *that they all may be one, as You, Father, are in Me, and I in You; that they also may be one in Us, that the world may believe that You sent Me.* [22] *And the glory which You gave Me I have given them, that they may be one just as We are one:* [23] *I in them, and You in Me; that they may be made perfect in*

one, and that the world may know that You have sent Me, and have loved them as You have loved Me."

The Antichrist will become one with his followers just as Jesus does with His and describes in John 17:11, *"that they may be one as We are."* He will also counterfeit Jesus in John 17:26, which reads: *"And I have declared to them Your name, and will declare it, that the love with which You loved Me may be in them, and I in them."* The recipient of the mark will be in the Antichrist and he will be in them." The mark of the Beast will help him take the role of God the Father, Son and Holy Ghost in the life of his subject.

17

Quantum Computers-666 the Image and Mark of the Beast

"Quantum computers are expected to be able to solve, in a few minutes, problems that are unsolvable by the supercomputers of today and tomorrow. This, in turn, will seed breakthroughs in the design of chemical processes, new materials, such as higher temperature superconductors, and new paradigms in machine learning and artificial intelligence.

Universal quantum computers will be available with computational power at a level of performance that will exceed even the most powerful classical computers of the future. They will be reprogrammable machines used to solve demanding computational problems, such as optimization tasks, database searches, machine learning and image recognition.

D-Wave Founder and Chief Scientist for its quantum computer, Eric Ladizinsky quoted Paul Davis who stated, "The nineteenth century was known as the machine age, the twentieth century will go down in history as the information age. I believe the 21st century will be the quantum age."

Quantum computing is going to merge with artificial intelligence and robotics and we will see it utilized in the image and mark of the Beast.

A quantum computer will be the ultimate for the Antichrist's police state. In science writer Julian Cribb's article, "Quantum Computing and the Dawn of the Quantum Tyranny.'

He stated, "every bit of data ever gathered on us can be recorded, stored, mined, sorted and retrieved by anyone with access and a 'Qaputer'…Artificial intelligence will scan this data constantly for patterns that might identify you as a 'subject of interest' – whether to police, intelligence services …Then there is your electronic trail – everywhere you went with your smart phone, satnav vehicle or tablet. Every email, text, tweet, Facebook entry, computer document or key stroke you ever made will be documented in your metadata, and its content can be retrieved."

Crib concluded, "They will be quietly identified, swept up and hushed before they can cause trouble…We have blithely 'assumed' quputers will always be used for good, when the probability is that they will also be used for evil."

A quantum computer fits perfectly with the technology god described in the book of Daniel that will have god like capabilities and will rule over many.

Quantum computers will also merge with AI and robotics and these computers will give the Antichrist all he needs. It should be noted that in the verse is the use of the word "them" will rule over many, could mean that there is more than one type of technology that will be employed by the Antichrist for the image and mark of the Beast, or it can also mean multiples of the same.

I. D-Wave and Demons-The Bible - demons are in the idols

The Bible makes it clear that demons are in the idols, consider these verses:

Leviticus 17:7, *"They shall no longer offer their sacrifices to the demons after which they play the harlot. This shall be a statute forever to them throughout their generations."*

Deuteronomy 32:17, "*They sacrificed to demons who were not God, To gods whom they have not known, New gods who came lately, Whom your fathers did not dread.*"

Psalm 106:37, *"They even sacrificed their sons and their daughters to the demons."*

Bible Basics "Demons" states, "It is significant that the Greek version of the Old Testament (the Septuagint) used the word 'daimonion' for "idol" in Dt. 32:17 and Ps. 106:37; this is the word translated "demon" in the New Testament."

It is a biblical teaching that demons reside in idols. This means that scientific ventures such as CERN, FAST and quantum computers can be influenced by demons.

What I want to note about quantum computers is that they:

Operate in an extreme environment
50,000 times weaker than the Earth's magnetic field
In very low pressure 10B times lower than atmospheric pressure
Are very delicate, and have to operate in a complete vacuum.
150x colder than interstellar space, the coldest place in the universe

What stood out is the extreme cold a quantum computer must operate from. Demonic spirits emit a chill unlike a cold you have ever felt anywhere else. We know that they reside in the air and can inhabit human bodies and inanimate objects. They like water and are extremely cold.

You can also see their eyes through the eyes of an oppressed or possessed human being. We know that they cause all kinds of influence and oppression and their mission is to steal, kill and destroy, and they lie and deceive. They also cause physical problems.

Satan heads them and directly under Satan is Death and Hades. Under them are demons of every hierarchy that oversee countries and cities.

II. Quantum Computers-its link to Satan and 666

We know that 666 is the son of Satan and the Antichrist is inhabited by Satan. The Antichrist will use technology, and the mark of the Beast is an idol inhabited or influenced and brought about by Satan.

Thus he inhabits the quantum computer that becomes the mark of the Beast and is also at work in the technology preparing it for his son.

A quantum processer uses quantum effects to explore many directions at once and tunnel through the hills. Scientists are not quite sure how they work.

A 300 qubit register could hold more numbers simultaneously than there are atoms in the known universe. Quantum computers have access with the parallel world in what is called tunneling. This is the slippage between universes. The one the math works for is that it is in two different universes at the same time. Quantum tunneling is the linking between those universes according to those who design the machine.

This report has already established the parallel universe, its details and its aim. This is what is powering the knowledge of the quantum computer. As a side note, the Bible emphasizes Satan's knowledge and wisdom in several passages such as the King of Tyre and Babylon.

This is also alluded to in Revelation 13:4, *"So they worshiped the dragon who gave authority to the Beast; and they worshipped the beast saying, "Who is like the beast: Who is able to make war with him?"*

Notice that in the Revelation the Antichrist is always referred to as the Beast, because he is brutal, savage and ferocious in the eyes of God, devouring souls. Thus Satan himself resides in this technology and establishes it for his son.

III. Nebuchadnezzar's Image of Cubits Vs. Quantum Computer Qubits

The parallel of the image of the Beast is Nebuchadnezzar's idolatrous image in Daniel Chapter 3. This image was 60 cubits high and six cubits wide. Quantum computers use qubits. A cubit with a c, is an ancient measurement of length, while in quantum computing a qubit with a q, is a unit of quantum information, which is a two-state quantum mechanical system, that essentially allows it to be in two places at the same time. Coincidence concerning the parallel? I don't think so.

It could possibly be that 666 could be the number of quantum bits or some type of measurement of the qubits that will go in people. In that demons are in the idols and the Dragon himself is in this one, you will literally be taking the number of the Antichrist's name because the image of the Beast honors the Son of Satan.

IV. The Revelation's Fractal Sequence -777 vs. 666 and Quantum Computing

In the book of Revelation, in the judgments is a triple seven. Jesus opens the seven seals and releases them with the seventh seal launching the seven trumpet judgements and the seventh trumpet releasing the seven bowl judgements. With the fifth trumpet is the first woe, the sixth trumpet: the second woe and the third woe coincides with the launching of the seven bowl judgements. The triple seven denotes God's final 21 plagues that end this world.

What needs to be noted is the fractal type repeating pattern of the plagues. Note that each set of seven open into another seven plagues and the final woes expand the fractal pattern of the last three of the final seven and each of these is not in the order as presented. Such as the sixth seal occurs after the trumpet and bowl judgments. The seventh seal is silence in heaven for a half an hour after the judgements and end of the Earth are completed. This appears to be a fractal that expands vs. the patterns in nature that decrease and become smaller. We see here that the God of the universe who created the world with this pattern throughout, would destroy it with the same. While this fractal enlarges it also ends vs. continuous repeating. It is noteworthy that the judgements are presented as a fractal that opens into the next branch.

666 is our second triple number only the numbers have no sequence of replication like the triple seven judgements in fractal depiction. The numbers themselves have a fractal like appearance with 700 the larger, 70 the smaller and seven the even smaller. Likewise the same with 666 only this number represents the Antichrist.

The 666 we see in Nebuchadnezzar's vision, was a double six of 60 cubits high, six cubits wide and added by a third six of six musical instruments sounding and we find the third six in the number of instruments that sound in symphony with all kinds of music. We already know that 666 is the number of idolatry and of an idol that Satan indwells, but how is the music significant? The third six releases sounds of six musical instruments. All music equates to math and there are also fractal patterns in music. This is a hint that the mark of the Beast will be numerical, and we know that Satan counterfeits God and the Trinity. We also see the fractals in the music that worship Nebuchadnezzar's image and according to an article that appeared in physicals world, in the quantum realm are fractal patterns. These fractals are to mimic God and mock Him and try to stand in place of Him by the Antichrist.

The Antichrist's reign comes under the 1st seal, which launches the four horsemen of the Apocalypse, not as a single judgement but setting the stage for the series of judgements and also as part of them.

In this report I have established that to be numbered, is to be numbered for death, that 666 equates with idolatry, and also with the unholy trinity. From Nebuchadnezzar's image we glean the Beast's image will comprise of mathematical equations meaning that it will be a technological number, that Satan himself possesses. Finally, it is the number of a man, because in the end that is all he is, a man and not God, but a man who is indwelled by Satan and who dares to be like God and who in the end will dwell in hell for eternity. He will be thrown bodily into the lake of fire.

18

Taking the Mark of the Beast-The Unforgivable Sin of Blasphemy Against the Holy Spirit

Christians for years have asked and inquired about the sin of blasphemy against the Holy Spirit, wondering if they could have possibly committed this sin, and debated who did commit this unforgivable sin that Jesus said would never be forgiven. Some theologians concluded it was refusing Jesus Christ as personal savior. There have been debates over if the sin can be committed in the age of grace, and how is it committed?

Blasphemy against the Holy Spirit is mentioned in the Gospels of Matthew and Mark, while Jesus was casting out demons. The Pharisees accused Jesus of casting them out by Beelzebub, the prince of demons. What could be more blasphemous than accusing Jesus of having a demon.

Jesus stated in response in Matthew 12:32, *"Whoever speaks a word against the Son of Man will be forgiven, but whoever speaks against the Holy Spirit will not be forgiven, either in this age or in the one to come."*

This story is also recapped in Mark and Jesus states in response in

Mark 3:27-28, *"Truly I tell you, the sons of men will be forgiven all sins and blasphemies, as many as they utter. But he who blasphemes against the Holy Spirit never has forgiveness, but is subject to eternal condemnation."*

In both of these passages Jesus provides insights into Satan's kingdom by stating in Matthew 12: 25-28:

²⁵ And Jesus knew their thoughts, and said unto them, Every kingdom divided against itself is brought to desolation; and every city or house divided against itself shall not stand:
²⁶ And if Satan cast out Satan, he is divided against himself; how shall then his kingdom stand?
²⁷ And if I by Beelzebub cast out devils, by whom do your children cast them out? therefore they shall be your judges.
²⁸ But if I cast out devils by the Spirit of God, then the kingdom of God is come unto you.

Jesus is telling us here that in Satan's kingdom demons enter into people and by the Holy Spirit they are cast out.

The third time blasphemy against the Holy Spirit is mentioned is in the Gospel of Luke and it is in a different context. Luke 12:4-11 provides a setting that is in the context of persecution. Luke 12:4-5 reads:

⁴ "And I say to you, My friends, do not be afraid of those who kill the body, and after that have no more that they can do. ⁵ But I will show you whom you should fear: Fear Him who, after He has killed, has power to cast into hell; yes, I say to you, fear Him!

This verse is essentially telling the believer to fear God and not man and what man can do to them.

⁶ "Are not five sparrows sold for two copper coins? And not one of them is forgotten before God. ⁷ But the very hairs of your head are all numbered. Do not fear therefore; you are of more value than many sparrows.

This next verse reiterates the value God has on the believer. One questions God's love and value for them during times of persecution, tribulation or tumultuous and difficult life circumstances. Jesus adds:

⁸ "Also I say to you, whoever confesses Me before men, him the Son of Man also will confess before the angels of God. ⁹ But he who denies Me before men will be denied before the angels of God.

While each of these verses apply to all of our lives at any time, we are looking at them in the context of persecution. It is obvious that while being persecuted there will come the moment when the believer will confess Christ before men. Jesus affirms that He will also confess their names before angels. Jesus also warns that if they deny knowing Him, He will deny knowing them. The next verse is the warning of blasphemy against the Holy Spirit, which may seem like it does not fit. Notice the next verse.

¹⁰ "And anyone who speaks a word against the Son of Man, it will be forgiven him; but to him who blasphemes against the Holy Spirit, it will not be forgiven.

After this verse, we have more on the persecution. The next verse reads:

¹¹ "Now when they bring you to the synagogues and magistrates and authorities, do not worry about how or what you should answer, or what you should say. ¹² For the Holy Spirit will teach you in that very hour what you ought to say."

Blasphemy against the Holy Spirit will be committed by taking the mark of the Beast. We see that when the mark is refused the next verse tells them that they will go before authorities, but the Holy Spirit will teach them in that hour what they ought to say.

Notice also the correlation with Revelation 3:5, which speaks of the denial and adds that their name is blotted out of the book of life signifying a loss of salvation to those who started out as believers and then denied Christ and took the mark. Revelation 3:5 states:

⁵He who overcomes shall be clothed in white garments, and I will not blot out his name from the Book of Life; but I will confess his name before My Father and before His angels.

The mark of the Beast is the ultimate idolatry and mimics the Trinity, and especially the Holy Spirit. It blasphemes and desecrates the Holy Spirit in the process.

Jesus in the Gospels spoke to Christians in two dispensations; those in the age of grace and also the Tribulation believers. He tells them in Matthew 24:13, that those who endure to the end will be saved. Because, by taking the mark they commit the unforgivable sin of blasphemy against the Holy Spirit.

The age of grace ends with the Rapture of the Church and the start of the Tribulation. It also begins the final seven years of the 70 weeks of Daniel 9:24 of desolations on Jerusalem.. This ushers in a dispensation of salvation that can be lost or prevented via the blasphemy of the Holy Spirit, which would result from taking the mark of the Beast.

I. Abomination of Desolation-Blasphemy of the Holy Spirit

The unique phrase "abomination of desolation," is used numerous times by Jesus as a warning. It is foretold by Daniel the prophet of the moment that the Antichrist declares himself as God and sets up his technological counterpart to the Trinity in the Holy of Holies. It is also called by Daniel in Daniel 8:3, *"the transgression of desolation."* The verse in its entirety reads: *"Then I heard a saint speaking and another saint said unto that certain saint which spoke, How long shall be the vision concerning the daily sacrifice and the transgression of desolation to give both the sanctuary and the host to be trodden under foot?"*

It is possible that the "transgression of desolation" is blasphemy of the Holy Spirit, which is so grievous a sin that it even puts a stop to the healing and cleansing power of the blood of Jesus Christ. Satan knows this fact, which is why it is part of his reign on the earth. His mark guarantees him the person's soul and that they would have no hope of redemption.

The reason for this is that the Spirit is a part of the redemption process, and is so Holy that when the Spirit is blasphemed, it cannot do its work but must retreat for the sake of its own glory because it is part of the glory of God.

Revelation 13:6 tells us that the Antichrist blasphemes God, it states, *"Then he opened his mouth in blasphemy against God, to blaspheme His name, His tabernacle, and those who dwell in heaven."* In line with his actions the Antichrist also institutes the mark of the Beast, which blasphemes the Holy Spirit and those who take the mark will commit the unforgivable sin of blasphemy against the Holy Spirit.

Scholars concluded that that the expression "abomination of desolation" referred to the desecration of the Second Temple by Antiochus IV Epiphanes, who erected a Zeus statue within the sacred areas. We see the grievous idolatry committed in the Temple by the Israelites in Ezekiel 6-9 bringing God's judgements onto the nation, but there is no association with the phrase in the book of Daniel because *"the transgression of desolation"* is even greater than just idolatry within the temple.

Daniel 9:27, adds:

²⁷ Then he shall confirm a covenant with many for one week;
But in the middle of the week
He shall bring an end to sacrifice and offering.
And on the wing of abominations shall be one who makes desolate,
Even until the consummation, which is determined,
Is poured out on the desolate."

The word for desolate is a word, which means put to silence, places laid waste, in ruins. It also means to astonish, to stun. The desolation is both literal and spiritual. The abomination of desolation is a term that not only speaks of a literal desolation due to the siege of Jerusalem, but a spiritual one as well due to the retreat of the Holy

Spirit from the Third Temple and the lives of those who take the mark of the Beast.

Earlier in this report I referred to Ezekiel 9 because God marked those who were to be sparred His judgement and as a counter to God we see the Antichrist sealing those who are his and persecuting believers. The Antichrist knows his believers are sealed unto him because by taking his mark they blaspheme the Holy Spirit and partake in the transgression of desolation.

II. The Mysterious Restrainer Removed Via Blasphemy of the Holy Spirit

The idea of the Holy Spirit blasphemed by the Antichrist during the Tribulation and his followers committing the sin by taking the mark of the Beast solves the mystery of the "restrainer removed," passage in 2 Thessalonians 2:2-12. The verses read:

2 Now, brethren, concerning the coming of our Lord Jesus Christ and our gathering together to Him, we ask you, ² not to be soon shaken in mind or troubled, either by spirit or by word or by letter, as if from us, as though the day of Christ had come. ³ Let no one deceive you by any means; for that Day will not come unless the falling away comes first, and the man of sin is revealed, the son of perdition, ⁴ who opposes and exalts himself above all that is called God or that is worshiped, so that he sits as God in the temple of God, showing himself that he is God.
*⁵ Do you not remember that when I was still with you I told you these things? ⁶ And now you know what is restraining, that he may be revealed in his own time. ⁷ **For the mystery of lawlessness is already at work; only He who now restrains will do so until He is taken out of the way.** ⁸ And then the lawless one will be revealed, whom the Lord will consume with the breath of His mouth and destroy with the brightness of His coming. ⁹ The coming of the lawless one is according to the working of Satan, with all power, signs, and lying wonders, ¹⁰ and with all unrighteous deception among those who perish, because they did not receive the love of the truth, that they might be saved. ¹¹ And for this reason God will send them strong delusion, that they should believe the lie, ¹² that they all may be condemned who did not believe the truth but had pleasure in unrighteousness.*

While it has been erroneously assumed that this passage refers to the Rapture and the Holy Spirit departing with the Saints in the Rapture, it is possible that the Holy Spirit retreats when blasphemed for the sake of its own glory. This is why it is an unforgivable sin because the sin would put a stop to the actions of the Holy Spirit in the areas it is blasphemed. By taking the mark, the taker blasphemes the Holy Spirit, a sin so great, the redemption power of the cross is nullified and cannot do its work.

III. 666 The Number of Blasphemy of the Holy Spirit

All of the technologies are in place to fulfill the mark of the Beast prophecies. This reveals the amazing accuracy of the prophetic writings in predicting the events of the end times.

Bible prophecy watchers never anticipated the Tower of Babel mentality of scientists that would reemerge in these end times, leading the way for the Antichrist.

It is clear in this report how technology will be used for Satan to directly oppose Jesus Christ and mimic the Holy Trinity and that Satan is influencing the discovery of those technologies.

We also see the merging of the parallel world through the mark of the Beast as the Antichrist will mimic the Trinity by marking the person with his name, entering and becoming one with and guiding them and by so doing will commit the unforgivable sin of blaspheming the Holy Spirit. He will also cause those who take the mark of the Beast to commit this unpardonable sin, and guarantee their eternal damnation.

It helps explain the significance of the number for a name as the act itself marks the Antichrist for eternal death from his birth. It also lends to the forecast that he will commit the ultimate blasphemous act for which there is no redemption and cause others to follow him in this deed.

Once a person takes the mark and blasphemes the Holy Spirit, there is no chance to turn back and no hope of redemption. If they did know Jesus Christ as savior the Spirit will depart and their name will be blotted out of the book of life. For those who refuse the mark, the Holy Spirit will be with them entirely giving them all that they should say when they go before those who will take their lives for their refusal of taking the mark.

For those of us who remain prior to the Rapture, this report should come as a warning of how close we actually are and how the days until the start of the Tribulation are few. If you don't know Jesus Christ as your personal savior now is the time to take Him into your heart and life. If you are a Christian, the days remaining to serve Him are running out and you will want to make the most of the days that remain.

For my brothers and sisters who might access this report during the Tribulation, it is clear why you must not take the mark.

From the moment of the abomination of desolation the times will be unprecedented in their evil, which will include the rampant blasphemy of the Holy Spirit. Going against Christ and accepting the mark You will commit the unforgivable sin of blasphemy against the Holy Spirit and by so doing will gain at most three and a half years of physical life during a time in which the Revelation plagues are in full force. One of the plagues affects those who have taken the mark, with grievous foul and loathsome sores (Rev. 16:2). Added to this will be the suffering caused by the bowl judgements; scorching sun that will burn your flesh and all bodies of water turning to blood and killing all of the life within among other judgements.

Although those who refuse the mark will suffer for a short time, from trying to live in a society where they cannot purchase any food or shelter, and being hunted by military and betrayed by family members and rounded up for torture and death; they will have the promise of eternal life with Christ. It will not be as torturous as the pain inflicted on those who take the mark, they will suffer the greater plagues on this Earth, and eternity in the lake of fire.

BIBLIOGRAPHY

THEOLOGY
Bible Basics-Demons
http://www.christadelphians.com/biblebasics/0603demons.html
Three woes what should we learn
http://lifehopeandtruth.com/prophecy/revelation/three-woes/
Ezekiel 28 Lucifer
https://www.biblegateway.com/passage/?search=Ezekiel%2028
How to count the mark of the Beast
http://www.nicholson1968.com/how-to-count-the-mark-of-the-beast.html

QUANTUM COMPUTING
Quantum Computing AI and More
http://www.techtimes.com/articles/165177/20160615/quantum-computing-ai-and-more-how-the-future-of-technology-is-shaping-up-as-per-andy-rubin.htm
Quantum computing and the dawn of the quantum tyranny
http://www.smh.com.au/comment/dawn-of-the-quantum-tyranny-20160108-gm1tay.html
Quantum computing and 3 dangerous predictions
http://forbiddenknowledgetv.net/Quantum-Computing-and-Three-Dangerous-Predictions/#comment-1933
Quantum Journey - D-Wave Chief Scientist, Eric Ladizinsky
https://www.youtube.com/watch?v=fArXhQBLDWE
Quantum Computing – Artificial Intelligence Is Here
https://www.youtube.com/watch?v=PqN_2jDVbOU
D-Wave Founder Eric Ladizinsky-The Coming Quantum Computing Revolution
https://www.youtube.com/watch?v=PUlYV--lLAA
Not Magic Quantum D Wave 2 X Mandela Effects
Quantum Manifesto
Quantum Computing, Google, CERN, NASA and the Mandela

Effect
https://www.youtube.com/watch?v=By56IOSZ7KY
Eric Ladizinsky: Quantum computing will be the next big revolution | WIRED 2014 | WIRED
https://www.youtube.com/watch?v=bLJ38KDS4Pc
Quantum Manifesto-A New Era of Technology
http://qurope.eu/system/files/u567/Quantum%20Manifesto.pdf

PARALLEL UNIVERSES
Parallel world Biblical?
http://www.space.com/32728-parallel-universes.html
Magnetic Fields
https://www.drpawluk.com/education/introduction-to-magnetic-field-therapy/
There's parallel universes http://www.space.com/32728-parallel-universes.html
Parallel Universes: Theories & Evidence
http://www.space.com/32728-parallel-universes.html

FRACTALS and MATHEMATICS
Math is hiding in the music we love
http://www.futurity.org/theres-math-hiding-in-the-music-we-love/
Fractal patterns in the quantum realm
http://physicsworld.com/cws/article/news/2010/feb/09/fractal-patterns-spotted-in-the-quantum-realm

SINGULARITY
Michio Kaku & Ray Kurzweil - Singularity is Close!
Cuckoo for Kaku
https://www.youtube.com/watch?v=qSUo9IEcYUUProf. Jürgen Schmidhuber - True Artificial Intelligence Will Change Everything
Singularity Lectures
https://www.youtube.com/watch?v=XkltShNd6XE
Do You Believe in God? | Ray Kurzweil Q & A | Singularity University
https://www.youtube.com/watch?v=-JvfdmPp3d8

TRANSHUMANISM-ARTIFICIAL INTELLIGENCE-

NANOTECHNOLOGY-CYBORGS

What if we could become transhumans? | Oskar Aszmann | TEDxVienna
https://www.youtube.com/watch?v=IyFR_ymj5x4
Our post human future David Simpson Ted Talks
https://www.youtube.com/watch?v=uAb-mSq615g
Humans, Cyborgs, Post humans: Francesca Ferrando at TEDx Silicon Alley Ted Talks
https://www.youtube.com/watch?v=RGjMUw03Bv0
A Trans human Manifesto What if we could become transhumans? | Oskar Aszmann | TEDxVienna TEDx Talks
https://www.youtube.com/watch?v=IyFR_ymj5x4
The coming trans human era: Jason Sosa at TEDx Grand Rapids Tedx Talks
https://www.youtube.com/watch?v=1Ugo2KEV2XQ
Transhumanism Artificial Intelligence and Nanotechnology Building Gods-Documentary
https://www.youtube.com/watch?v=dEGRJlSNppoHow Will Nanotechnology Change the World ? - Full Documentary
STAR Documentaries
https://www.youtube.com/watch?v=cG9P8DLuh0U
Davos 2016 - The State of Artificial Intelligence
World Economic Forum
https://www.youtube.com/watch?v=VBceREwF7SA
Nick Bostrom: What happens when our computers get smarter than we are
https://www.youtube.com/watch?v=MnT1xgZgkpkw
2045 Initiative about http://2045.com/tech2/
2045 super elastic skin http://2045.com/news/34818.html
2045 Immortal.me http://www.immortal.me/
Ray Kurzweil can machines ever have souls
TEDx Talks
https://tech.slashdot.org/story/08/11/19/1334239/ray-kurzweil-wonders-can-machines-ever-have-souls
What will be the next big scientific breakthrough? | Eric Haseltine TED
https://www.youtube.com/watch?v=i1MRJrm9Gts
Dr. Aubrey de Grey - Ending Human Aging
Singularity Lectures

https://www.youtube.com/watch?v=6CdrIj238X8
Aubrey de Grey interviewed by Ray Kurzweil
https://www.youtube.com/watch?v=E3dFPyuJ4P0
Datun Center
https://www.youtube.com/channel/UCFLDZkc48xcVTQO1Hl4G7OA
Predictions for 2020s With Ray Kurzweil
Future Thinking
https://www.youtube.com/watch?v=YVfHCSJ9GSE
Ray Kurzweil - How technology will change the near future
Future Thinking
https://www.youtube.com/watch?v=SOg5lqpwcUo
Michio Kaku - Coming Breakthroughs
Dr. Kaku's Universe
https://www.youtube.com/watch?v=Rs6spycukN0
Design at the Intersection of Technology and Biology | Neri Oxman
TED Talks
https://www.youtube.com/watch?v=CVa_IZVzUoc
Ray Kurzweil - The Age Spiritual Machines (1999)
Singularity Lectures
https://www.youtube.com/watch?v=kLwvXz0kyxA
Ray Kurzweil: "How to Create a Mind" | Talks at Google
https://www.youtube.com/watch?v=zihTWh5i2C4Ray Kurzweil: We'll Become Godlike When We Connect Our Brains to The Cloud
The WorldPost
https://www.youtube.com/watch?v=uHg0FIilK0E
DigPhilosophy TED
https://www.youtube.com/user/TEDtalksDirector
Ray Kurzweil 2016 - What does the future look like - Ray Kurzweil
Science 2016
https://www.youtube.com/watch?v=wT25E7KDiPs
Ray Kurzweil - Genetics, Nanotechnology, and Robotics Will Create a Flat and Equitable World (2005)
Singularity Lectures
https://www.youtube.com/watch?v=FGBfAteH1Xs
The end of humanity: Nick Bostrom at TEDxOxford
TEDx Talks
https://www.youtube.com/watch?v=P0Nf3TcMiHo

How Close Are Humans to Immortality? By David Sinclair
Future Thinking
https://www.youtube.com/channel/UCYYDI1ZtMUpvF9syk5QTtYg
Darpa Cyborgs
http://www.thedailybeast.com/articles/2016/04/16/cyborgs-aren-t-just-for-sci-fi-anymore.html
Darpa Prepares to Unleash Storm of Gremlins
http://www.fool.com/investing/general/2016/04/16/darpa-prepares-to-unleash-storm-of-gremlins-us-fo.aspx?source=yahoo-2&utm_campaign=article&utm_medium=feed&utm_source=yahoo-2

BRAIN CHIPS
Brown University Creates First Wireless implanted brain computer interface
http://www.extremetech.com/extreme/149879-brown-university-creates-first-wireless-implanted-brain-computer-interface
Brain Chip Implant Uses Power of Thought
https://www.youtube.com/watch?v=vb3cPjkjbi4
Intel: Chips in Brains will control computers by 2020
http://www.computerworld.com/article/2521888/app-development/intel--chips-in-brains-will-control-computers-by-2020.html
Look out your medicine is watching you
http://www.foxnews.com/health/2010/11/09/smart-pill-embedded-microchip.html
Lab rats driven by remote control
http://www.theguardian.com/world/2002/may/02/animalwelfare.highereducation
How Smart Dust could spy on your brain
https://www.technologyreview.com/s/517091/how-smart-dust-could-spy-on-your-brain/
Neural dust implanted in the brain may let minds meld with machines
http://www.huffingtonpost.com/2013/07/17/neural-dust_n_3612307.html
Brain cells fused with computer chips
http://www.livescience.com/681-brain-cells-fused-computer-

chip.html
The potential of brain chips is limitless after man controls arm with his thoughts
https://www.washingtonpost.com/news/to-your-health/wp/2015/05/22/brain-chip-that-let-man-control-robot-arm-is-just-the-beginning-heres-a-look-at-the-future-of-implantable-chips/
I got a computer chip implanted in my hand and the rest of the world won't be far behind
http://www.techinsider.io/presidential-candidate-zoltan-istvan-gets-an-rfid-chip-implant-2015-9
Gold chip can now be implanted in the human brain
http://www.designntrend.com/articles/6228/20130718/gold-chip-now-implanted-human-brain.htm
Here's what the next brain chip will be made of
http://www.defenseone.com/technology/2014/10/heres-what-next-brain-implant-will-be-made/97190/
A surprising number of adults are open to brain chip implants
http://www.dailydot.com/technology/brain-chip-implants-internet/
How Much Longer Until We Become the Hive Mind
http://io9.gizmodo.com/how-much-longer-until-humanity-becomes-a-hive-mind-453848055
Saudi 'Killer Chip' Implant Would Track, Eliminate Undesirables
http://www.foxnews.com/story/2009/05/18/saudi-killer-chip-implant-would-track-eliminate-undesirables.html
Scientists Create Neural Dust that will connect man to machine
https://occupycorporatism.com/scientists-create-neural-dust-that-will-connect-man-to-machine/
Neuroscientist wants to upload humanity to computer
http://www.popsci.com/article/science/neuroscientist-who-wants-upload-humanity-computer
Human Brain Project-cofounded by EU
https://www.humanbrainproject.eu/2016-events
Human Computer Interaction series
http://eprints.eemcs.utwente.nl/17752/01/front-matter.pdf
Mind Control World Cache
http://www.mindcontrol.se/?page_id=5537
Synthetic Telepathy
http://www.synthetictelepathy.net/emerging-technologies/ethical-

issues-involved-in-hybrid-bionic-systems-research/
The Many ways Google wants to RFID chip your body
https://occupycorporatism.com/many-ways-google-wants-rfid-chip-body/

HOLOGRAMS
Gizmag Holograms
http://www.gizmag.com/mit-3d-projector-hologram/32111/
Upload your brain into a hologram
http://www.messagetoeagle.com/upload-your-brain-into-a-hologram-project-avatar-2045-a-new-era-for-humanity-or-scientific-madness/

DNA CRISPR
DNA Bits
http://www.coindesk.com/israels-dna-bits-moves-beyond-currency-with-genes-blockchain/
Gene coin
http://genecoin.me/index.html
DNA Coin desk
http://www.coindesk.com/israels-dna-bits-moves-beyond-currency-with-genes-blockchain/
Crispr to make a dragon or unicorn
http://pandawhale.com/post/69656/someone-will-eventually-use-crispr-to-try-to-make-a-dragon-or-unicorn
Cracking the Code of Life PBS Nova
https://www.youtube.com/watch?v=_IgSDVD4QEc&ebc=ANyPx
KoluNapsFjyekq6SimzyXQVm1uUzWMlte63vGydBXupItP3ObKZ
45QpUZcSq4DpzzbMxsTq9MOJp2Kgtd9lfJHUByxk3w
Alignment of gold clusters on DNA
http://www.ncbi.nlm.nih.gov/pubmed/19938825
Twitter Carbon Copies
https://twitter.com/carboncopiesorg
Hacking Life programing new functions bacteria
http://www.kurzweilai.net/hacking-life-how-to-program-new-functions-for-living-bacteria-and-yeast
Genome in a bottle

http://web.stanford.edu/group/jimb/cgi-bin/consortia/giab/

OTHER
The Last Places on Earth Without the Internet
http://www.bbc.com/future/story/20140214-the-last-places-without-internet
Biological Supercomputer uses the juice of life
http://www.computerworld.com/article/3040707/computer-hardware/biological-supercomputer-uses-the-juice-of-life.html
FAST: Largest Radio Telescope Open for Business
http://www.skyandtelescope.com/astronomy-blogs/astronomy-space-david-dickinson/fast-worlds-largest-radio-telescope-open/
Scientists offer quantum theory of soul's existence
http://www.news.com.au/tablet/quantum-scientists-offer-proof-soul-exists/story-fnenjnc3-1226507686757

EUROPEAN UNION
EU Commission Research and Innovation
http://ec.europa.eu/research/index.cfm
Qurope eu
http://qurope.eu/
Cordis
http://cordis.europa.eu/home_en.html
European Political Strategy Centre
http://ec.europa.eu/epsc/newsletter/nl-1-15.html

m/pod-product-compliance